BACK TO THE WORLD

BACK TO THE WORLD

A LIFE AFTER JONESTOWN

EUGENE SMITH

AS TOLD TO **ETHAN CASEY**

FORT WORTH, TEXAS

LIBRARY OF CONGRESS CATALOGING-IN-PUBLICATION DATA

Names: Smith, Eugene, 1957– author. | Casey, Ethan, 1965–
Title: Back to the world : a life after Jonestown / Eugene Smith ; as told to Ethan Casey.
Description: Fort Worth, Texas : TCU Press, [2021] | Summary: "Eugene Smith lost his mother, wife, and infant son in the mass murder-suicide at Jonestown, Guyana, on November 18, 1978. Repatriated by the US authorities on New Year›s Eve, he broke a $50 bill stashed in his shoe to buy breakfast for himself and a fellow survivor. Returning to California at age twenty-one, Smith faced the daunting challenge of building from scratch a meaningful and self-sufficient life in the American society he thought he had left behind. "My first responsibility as a survivor," he writes, "was not to embarrass my mother or my wife or my child, and to set an example that can›t be questioned." *Back to the World* is the story of a double survival: first of the destruction of the idealistic but tragically flawed Peoples Temple community, then of its aftermath. Having survived, Smith has hard questions for today's America'— Provided by publisher.
Identifiers: LCCN 2020051363 (print) | LCCN 2020051364 (ebook) | ISBN 9780875657783 (paperback) | ISBN 9780875657851 (ebook)
Subjects: LCSH: Smith, Eugene, 1957– | Jones, Jim, 1931–1978. | Peoples Temple—Biography. | Ex-cultists—California—Biography. | African American men—California—Biography. | Men—California—Biography. | Jonestown Mass Suicide, Jonestown, Guyana, 1978. | LCGFT: Autobiographies.
Classification: LCC BP605.P46 S65 2021 (print) | LCC BP605.P46 (ebook) | DDC 988.103/2092 [B]—dc23
LC record available at https://lccn.loc.gov/2020051363
LC ebook record available at https://lccn.loc.gov/2020051364

TCU Box 298300
Fort Worth, Texas 76129
To order books: 1.800.826.8911

Design by Julie Rushing

CONTENTS

FOREWORD

Most books about an already well-known event attempt telling readers for the umpteenth time what happened at a specific time and place without helping us learn *how* and *why* it occurred. History doesn't happen in a vacuum. When a book is published that provides fresh context, especially when it's written by someone who was there and personally involved, rather than a supposedly impartial observer, it deserves special respect. There aren't many of them. Eugene Smith's *Back to the World* is one of the best, and truest, that you'll ever read. Late on Saturday afternoon, November 18, 1978, he was working at Peoples Temples headquarters in Georgetown, Guyana, when a mass murder-suicide, orchestrated by Temple leader Jim Jones, took place in Jonestown, 250 miles away across near-impenetrable jungle. More than nine hundred men, women, and children died that day, including Jones, a US congressman, and Eugene Smith's wife and infant son. Afterward he and the other Temple staffers in Georgetown were held in brutal custody for weeks, suspected of comprising a hit squad intended to murder alleged Jones enemies. Smith's vivid, bitter memories of those terrible days shed critical light on a tragedy most people think they already know everything about.

Written with incredible fortitude and unusual bluntness, *Back to the World* also presents readers with insights revealing how Jones and Peoples Temple attracted intelligent, socially concerned individuals rather than weak-minded loyalists, and, in particular, appealed to young Black men in the turbulent 1960s and 1970s. We see the Temple and its demagogue leader through the critical eyes of an intelligent person who viewed Jones with considerable skepticism—many in the Temple did—but greatly valued the avowed Temple mission of bringing about a new American era of racial, gender, and economic equality. How Temple members collectively made that attempt, and why they failed, not only reflects their doomed struggle, but anticipates the ever-widening schisms of modern-day America. It makes for frequently uncomfortable reading, but honest reflection on painful facts isn't supposed to be easy.

Smith's post-Temple life is especially illuminating. He and a handful of survivors returned to a homeland, came "back to the world," where they had been instantly and irradicably branded as pariahs. They in turn mistrusted everyone, often including each other. The aftermath of Jonestown is as important to understand as the events that led to the awful events there. After you read this book, you'll know why.

And you'll know why Eugene Smith, so many years after 11/18/78, still feels compelled to share his story with you when, at the same time, he has learned to cherish anonymity. He's well aware of the contradiction, writing, "I want to be forgotten. The irony is that I'm writing a book so that you'll remember."

Remember, and better *understand*. We benefit from his honesty, and his courage.

Jeff Guinn, author of
The Road to Jonestown
Fort Worth, Texas
Spring 2021

A NOTE ON WORDS AND PICTURES

This book is my story. If you want thorough accounts of Peoples Temple and the mass murder-suicide that took place in Jonestown, Guyana, on November 18, 1978, and the closely related assassination of US Congressman Leo Ryan and four others at the airstrip at Matthews Ridge, there is a vast preexisting literature of other books you can read. Two that I recommend are *The Road to Jonestown* by Jeff Guinn and the oral history *Stories from Jonestown* by Leigh Fondakowski, which is a companion to the play she directed, *The People's Temple*, staged in Berkeley in 2005. For a shorter written account, I recommend the entry written by Rebecca Moore on the website of the World Religions and Spirituality Project (https://wrldrels.org/2016/10/08/peoples-temple/). I also recommend the 2006 documentary *Jonestown: The Life and Death of Peoples Temple*, directed by Stanley Nelson.

In any case, I can't tell the whole story, but I can tell my story. This book is my contribution. Part of its value is that it's the first book-length memoir of Peoples Temple and Jonestown by a Black man, despite the fact that some 70 percent of the 918 people who perished there were African American. But as you read, I think that you will find I had other good reasons for telling my story. One of those is that, more than forty years after Jonestown, the injustices that are ingrained in American society and politics—injustices that the Temple was a sustained attempt to address—have not gone away. If anything, they've only gotten worse and more deeply ingrained. As you can tell just by looking around your own city or turning on the television, they're still all around us and in our faces every day. The story of Peoples Temple and Jonestown, and my personal story, should help us understand why that is and what we ought to be doing about it.

Some names have been changed to protect the innocent. Those names that were changed were and are friends of mine. They have made the choice to leave this part of their lives behind them. I understand why, and I will respect that.

I want to thank a few people. Fielding "Mac" McGehee and Rebecca Moore prompted me, and Jeff Guinn promoted me to his friend Dan Williams, director of TCU Press. Dan deserves credit for wanting to publish my story after many other publishers rejected or ignored it, and for remaining steadfast in his advocacy and support. Many thanks to Dan and to the staff of TCU Press: Kathy Walton, Rebecca Allen, and Molly Spain. Dan Williams also introduced me to Ethan Casey, a professional writer and editor based in Seattle. One thing that led me to select Ethan as my collaborator is his experience living in and writing about other countries, including Haiti, Pakistan, South Africa, and Thailand. Like me, he returned to live in the United States after seeing it from afar. I have a lot of my own story inside my head, and I have a habit of over-describing things. Ethan assisted me in translating my story into a narrative that we hope will be both readable and edifying to readers whose life experiences are likely to be very different from mine. We often cautioned each other to avoid going down rabbit holes, as we put it. Ethan and I spent a week together in the Bay Area in July 2018, plus many hours on the phone before and since then, over more than two years.

I also want to give special thanks to Lynda Sykes and Denice Stephenson, who spent time on the phone with Ethan, as did Leigh Fondakowski and Mac McGehee. Jeb Wyman was generous with his time and editorial wisdom, offering feedback on a late draft, on short notice and a tight deadline. Jennifer Haywood was also helpful and supportive.

Finally, I want to explain why this book contains no photographs. The short answer is that this book has no pictures in it because I have none to offer. What I do have to offer are my story and my words. In Chapter 10, I describe how in the mid-2000s I spent weekends volunteering at the California Historical Society in San Francisco, assisting archivists in sifting through thousands of media and personal photographs of Peoples Temple and Jonestown, to identify some of the people in them. But the historical society has a policy of charging for use of materials in its collections, regardless of who you are, and I have a policy of not paying to use photos that I, as a survivor, should be entitled to use free of charge.

It's also true that I really don't have many visual images of my life. My wife Ollie, who died in Jonestown, had pictures, and those were either destroyed or kept from me. The US Department of State collected all paperwork that remained in Jonestown after the incident and never returned any of it to its rightful owners. You can imagine how I feel about that. When I returned to the United States, it was my intention to never again have a picture taken of myself. There are passport pictures, and there are some group pictures that I couldn't avoid being in. But other than that—well, you get the picture.

Eugene Smith

PART ONE

MY ROAD TO JONESTOWN

CHAPTER 1
The Whole World Thinks We're Nuts

November 18, 1978

We're at the movie theater in Georgetown, unwinding after a busy week, watching *Tora! Tora! Tora!* It's a night out. The usher comes down the aisle to tell us that there's been a shooting at Lamaha Gardens, Peoples Temple's home base in the Guyanese capital. We're taken aback. "What?" "Yeah, there's been a shooting at Lamaha Gardens."

So we all rush out. I think Mike Touchette is driving, and we get in the back of the Bedford truck and fly back across town. I'm thinking this can't be real. Something must have happened at the Guyanese Defence Force base, right across the street. Maybe it was an errant bullet, but surely nobody got shot.

We get to the house at Lamaha Gardens, and I jump out to go check for my best friend, Beau. I hear somebody calling me: "Gene, Gene." I look over into the elephant grass, and I see Beau and Robyn crouching by the fence.

"What's up?"

"They're killing the kids."

"What?"

"They're killing the kids upstairs."

I'm frozen, trying to take this in. "*We're* killing the kids? *Our* people are killing kids?"

"They're killing the kids upstairs, Gene."

"Look," I say. "Give me five minutes. If I'm not back in five minutes, go to the prime minister's house and claim asylum." We had carte blanche with Prime Minister Forbes Burnham, and we went to his house on a regular basis. He had a private zoo. We were free to walk the grounds of his residence. It was no problem, no security or anything. So us showing up at any time wouldn't be a big thing.

So I run upstairs and, as I come into the front room, the open space, I see these two senior citizens there, and my first impression is droopy-eyed hound dogs. That's how these seniors look, like they've been crying for days. I see people standing in the kitchen, and as I'm going down the hall, Ana, Tony Walker's wife, stops me and says, "Gene, don't go back there."

When you went into the master bedroom at Lamaha Gardens, when you opened the door, the door blocked the shower, so you had to step into the room and close the door. So I step into the room and close the door. And I look inside the shower, where the blood is, and it hasn't coagulated yet. There are Sharon Amos and her children Liane, Christa, and Martin, and their throats have been cut. I look at them. I take it in. I'm processing it. I'm not running. How come I'm not running? Who did this? I back into the hall, and it seems like I stood there forever, but I didn't. It's not even the full five minutes before I'm back downstairs. I walk out and look to my left, where the kitchen is when you exit the hallway into the main room. I see Chuck Beikman standing there. It hasn't yet occurred to me that he might be involved in this. I walk out, calmly, because I don't know who did it.

And was that the beginning—or was that the end? Obviously, the Guyanese Defence Force had not done these killings. Somebody in the house killed this woman and these children. Was it the beginning? In other words, were they given instructions to kill everybody? Or was this the end? They killed the children. I'm baffled by that, and at the same time I'm frightened, because I wasn't here when it happened. I wasn't a witness to it. But now I'm compromised, because they know that I know, and they can see me going out the door.

I had already seen Beau, outside in the elephant grass, before I went into the house. He had told me not to go in the house, but I had to. The reason I had to was that Christa, who was eleven years old, couldn't stand her own mother, Sharon Amos, so she had basically adopted my wife, Ollie. Sharon showed a distinct preference for Christa's brother, Martin, so she felt slighted. Ollie had looked out for Christa prior to becoming pregnant, and they had bonded. "Don't worry about your mother," Ollie would say to Christa. "It's okay. Everybody loves you. Don't worry about it. Come on, you can be part of my family." That's how it started out. Between Ollie and Christa, they adopted me back into my own family. Christa was there, at Lamaha Gardens, because her father had come to Guyana with the group called the Concerned Relatives and Congressman

Leo Ryan to check on his family, and he was in town waiting. He had not gone to the encampment at Jonestown. The Reverend Jim Jones, the Temple leader, had let Sharon and the children come to Georgetown. So I had gone upstairs to confirm that Christa was dead, because I had to tell Ollie. I had to go. I didn't really have a choice.

I walk back down, and I say, "We can't run. If we run, we're blamed. We had nothing to do with it, but we will be blamed. If we stay, it's a catch-22, but we know we didn't do it, because I wasn't here and you guys were downstairs. Everybody else is upstairs. We gotta pay the piper." So I help Teena back across the fence. Beau hops over. We're standing there waiting. I don't know what for. Just waiting. Nobody comes downstairs, and we don't go upstairs. The only people I trust are Robyn and Beau and the people who came over in the truck with me from the movie theater. That's it. I don't trust any of the others: Johnny Cobb, Stephan Jones, Jim Jones Jr., none of the basketball team. None of them.

The Guyanese police arrive soon after, and they rush in and start pushing everybody outside. They bring everybody downstairs and have everybody just stand outside. "We hear that you're killing people and you got people buried in the walls," they say. And they're going through everything: the wells, the cistern outside the house. I say, "We don't have any bodies buried. The only bodies are up there in the shower." Then they start the interrogations. The interrogations start out lightly, but as the hours go on, they get more aggressive.

Somebody has alerted the Guyanese Defence Force, so they arrive during the night of the eighteenth and set up an encampment around Lamaha Gardens, and none of the guns are pointing out. They're all pointing in. That's interesting, I think to myself. So they're not here to protect us. They're here to protect everybody else *from* us. What the fuck has happened? People are being interrogated all night and all day the next day, the nineteenth.

The investigator says to me, "What's your name?"

"Eugene Smith," I tell him.

"Do you know what happened?"

"I don't know."

"That's all I hear," he says. "'I don't know. I don't know. I don't know.' I'm tired of hearing 'I don't know.' Somebody knows something, and I want to know what you know."

"I wasn't here. I was at the movie theater."

"You know all these people?"

"Yes, I know all of them."

"What else do you know?"

"That's all I know. I came home. These people were dead already. I don't know anything."

"Who killed them?"

"I don't know."

Now this investigator is irate. He's screaming. He says, "You're not leaving here alive. If you want to kill yourself or kill each other, we don't care, but you killed Guyanese citizens." That's when I know for a fact that somebody has died in Jonestown.

They've already arrested Stephan Jones and taken him and a couple other people out to the prison. Daily they put us in a van and take us there. "Tell us the truth. If you don't tell us the truth, this is where you're gonna be at, so we want you to have a relationship with this prison. This is where you're gonna be. Get used to it. We're bringing you here now, but you're eventually gonna be living here." The only way you could recognize anybody at the prison was by their voice. With all the little layers of screen, you couldn't see the person that you were talking to. So, when we went out to visit people, you didn't know who they were unless you knew their voice. You couldn't see them. Our prisons here in the US are high-grade condominiums compared to prisons in Guyana. Dirt floor, open roof, mystery meals. Sometimes your meal was still moving when you got it. And they weren't very happy with us because, as far as they were concerned, we had killed Guyanese citizens. "If you crazy Americans want to kill yourselves, you fucking Yankees, that's fine, but you killed Guyanese citizens. You're gonna pay for that."

We find out that the State Department and the US military have arrived, and that they're airlifting medical equipment. They say, "We found a few people, but not that many." The interrogation goes on into the next day, the twentieth of November. "We found some adults and some children," the interrogator tells us. We find out now that Tim Carter, Stanley Clayton, Odell Rhodes, and Leslie Wilson and Jakari, my friend Joe Wilson's wife and son, escaped. They showed up probably on the twenty-first. Between the twentieth and the twenty-first, we're hearing that they found bodies in the bush around the perimeter of

Jonestown. We heard that some of those had been shot and that the trees had been sprayed with bullets chest and waist high, although this was later refuted.

So I hold out hope. I know Ollie wouldn't take the poison. I know she would die for Martin, our infant son. On the other hand, I knew from the first night I arrived in Jonestown eight months ago, in March 1978, that my mother would never return to the United States. She was completely engrossed in Peoples Temple, and she couldn't return to the US. In Peoples Temple, we didn't call our elders old people. We were discouraged from doing that. We called them seniors, and they were seen as the repositories of knowledge and held in high esteem. When you have a senior in her sixties or seventies, and these children are catering to her, there's no way she's going to want to return to the US, because here they don't give a shit about you if you're a senior citizen. In American society, you lose value as you get older. In Peoples Temple, you gained value.

For three days I hold out hope that Ollie has escaped. And then, on the twenty-first, the GDF comes back and tells us everybody in Jonestown is dead. I'm standing up on the balcony at Lamaha Gardens, with Robyn and Joan Pursley. Everybody's gone. There are no more survivors. The people that escaped escaped, but for all intents and purposes, everybody's dead. Over the days since November 18 they found bodies, and it turned out those bodies were on top of other bodies, and underneath those were the bodies of children. For a long time, they didn't know how many bodies there were. There's no TV, no radio. We had to wait for somebody to come back, and then the government approached the Jones boys, and they were going to go back into Jonestown and do some identifications. I was mad. I was like, "Why them? Why not us? Why don't we all go back? Why just them?" I was beyond angry. Everybody should go. But they didn't have a contingency to control all seventy survivors, taking them back into the bush, and they didn't know what we were going to do.

So the Jones boys went back and, quite naturally, identified their own father and mother. We're all, "Okay, be sure to look for So-and-so. Tell me if you see Ollie. Tell me if you see So-and-so." When I saw the pictures, weeks later, I could see that there was no way they could identify the bodies, because in the ninety-degree weather, 85 to 90 percent humidity, the bodies were swelling within hours and bursting within a day. The US military, sent in to recover the bodies, didn't know how to pack them to get them back to the US. They finally just started packing the bodies in aluminum caskets to carry them back, and they tried to refrigerate them.

I'm trying to figure this out. I don't know who to trust. There's no one to ask for help. We know that people escaped. We don't know how they were able to escape, or who all of them are. We know that Tim Carter, his brother Mike, and Mike Prokes emerged from the jungle with a crazy story of burying approximately half a million dollars in a suitcase. We know that Leslie Wilson escaped, but it took her forever to get through the bush and along the railroad track to Matthews Ridge, with her infant son. The Bogue and Parks families escaped by coming out of Jonestown with Congressman Ryan. Odell Rhodes and Stanley Clayton stayed in Jonestown but escaped the carnage and are now across town, being held at different places. They're all scared of us, because their assumption is that the quote "basketball team" was actually a hit team for anybody that escaped. They thought the basketball team was tasked with doing whatever was necessary to make sure nobody got back to the US. Some kind of way Odell Rhodes gets in his head that they had heard Stephan Jones tell me, Eugene Smith, "Make sure nobody gets off any plane going back to the USA." So I ended up being held in the country even longer because of that. But what the basketball team actually was was a group of fifteen or so friends, centered around the Jones boys, who had an affinity for basketball. I liked basketball, but I never played with them, because in my mind basketball was a way for them to avoid having to work. I was resentful of them, so anything they did, I didn't do.

I had been assigned at the end of August to replace Billy Oliver as the customs agent for Peoples Temple in Georgetown. The Temple leadership thought Billy was not clearing enough materiel through Guyanese customs in a timely manner. Basically, the Temple was bringing stuff into the country that they didn't want looked at too closely. As of November 18 I had been in Georgetown, doing this customs work, for about two and a half months. Towards the end of that period, Sharon

Amos and Debbie Touchette had been preoccupied negotiating with the Concerned Relatives, who wanted reassurance that their loved ones in Jonestown were safe and not being held against their will. They had recruited Congressman Leo Ryan of California and were planning to visit Jonestown with him to see for themselves. Jones was opposed to their visit and tried to prevent it, and for that reason the congressman and the Concerned Relatives cooled their heels in Georgetown for about a week and negotiated. Congressman Ryan was very focused and had a lot of confidence, or arrogance, or ignorance—I'm not sure which—and he ended up making the Jonestown visit happen. But it ended up being the straw that broke the camel's back. Meanwhile, Sharon and Debbie's preoccupation with Ryan's impending visit had given me more freedom than I would usually have, to get on with my own customs work and planning without them looking over my shoulder.

I never saw my mom after I went into Georgetown, and I didn't communicate with her at all. From the night I first arrived in Jonestown, in March, I had known my mom was just glazed over. No matter what would've happened, she could not have returned to the US. I had no way of taking care of her. She was fifty-three when she adopted me, so now she was seventy-four. It would not have been impossible for her to get by in the US on social services, but it would've been so much more difficult. I must be coming off as really uncaring by saying this, but it's not like that.

My concern was Ollie, my wife. Later, when I accessed my FBI file through the Freedom of Information Act, I learned that members of the Planning Commission, or PC, the governing body of Peoples Temple, had stated, "We only trust Eugene in times of crisis." That was true, because Ollie came first. For a lot of people, that wasn't the case. For them Jones came first, or the cause came first. For me, Ollie came first. I'd been in Lamaha Gardens, without Ollie, since August. I had decided on my very first night in Jonestown that I had to get out, but I had not been able to figure out how to get out with my family. I had turned twenty-one in Jonestown, on July 29, and I went to Georgetown at the end of August or the beginning of September. Billy Oliver had to spend a week or so showing me the ropes and introducing me to his contacts in the Guyanese ministries and at the port. Then I had to create my own system of communicating with these men and women. Everybody had their own style. Billy was a couple years younger than me. I don't know how I was chosen. I don't understand it, other than that there was a fear. They sent the basketball team away from Jonestown, and they sent me, Robyn, Joan, Laura—people you wouldn't see outwardly as a danger. What you would see is that these people could see past their noses. Jim Jones might have been thinking, "Do I trust them, or do I put them in a position of importance and let them just stay out of the way?"

What Jones always did was split the family. That kept you from running. Ollie was a singer. Her family had sung gospel. Her mother and younger brother were both singers. When I left Jonestown to come into Georgetown to do customs, I was assured that Ollie would come to town in six weeks or so to sing for the prime minister, and that she would bring the baby with her. I said, "I need this promise, otherwise I'm not going." I wasn't actually in a position to say I wasn't going, because they made it quite clear: "You're going. If you don't go, there's issues." When they say issues, that means that, "Your wife, oh, she's gonna work her ass off. She's not gonna be in the nursery anymore, she's gonna be in the field. We'll have somebody else watch your baby while she's out there working hard." It's like, "Yeah, I guess I'm going." But my idea was that Ollie would come into town, sing for the prime minister, and then, when she left that stage, she was going to the embassy, her and Martin and me.

Whenever you left Jonestown going somewhere, Jones would always have a story of why you left. "Oh, he's avenging Father, he's doing this, she's doing that." He always put a paranoid spin on it: "No matter who you are, you'll always be associated with Peoples Temple. You'll never live that down." People thought that the people who left Jonestown on assignments for Jones were his most trusted people, but it wasn't like that. They were the people he was scared of, people he was afraid would organize, would fight back, would resist. The basketball team was Stephan, Jimmy, John, and their friends. They had gone to California with Jones, thirteen years earlier, from the original Temple in Indianapolis. So they knew Jones for who he really was, not for what we thought he was or thought we saw. Stephan would confront him. Jones's wife Marceline would typically step in and say, "Okay. Let's just calm it down a little bit." But the only people that would challenge him were all away from Jonestown on November 18. The people that were left would not challenge Jones in any fashion.

It was almost like it was prearranged: "I need these people gone. If anything happens, I need to be able to control the situation." We already had our suicide drills, which people didn't particularly like. Drinking a flavored concoction. "You just drank poison." Forced drills and voluntary drills. What made things almost normal was one little phrase: "revolutionary suicide." Revolutionary suicide justified the ends. Most Christians understand that suicide is a no-no; you don't do that. In Jim Jones's interpretation of revolutionary suicide it's accepted because, rather than have your seniors or your children tortured, you choose to take their lives as well as your own, and leave the enemy with no one to kill. Jones said it was a Huey Newton thing. He had met Huey Newton, cofounder of the Black Panthers, in Cuba, but Jones twisted its original meaning. And it made a lot of people uncomfortable. It's like, "Screw that. There is no justified reason for suicide. You fight to the end. If you get killed, you get killed. If you don't, you don't. But you don't commit suicide." Yet and still, a lot of people did commit suicide in Jonestown. But I also know that when the GDF soldiers and some of the doctors came back, they found people who had been injected in all parts of their bodies, as if they had been running after them to inject them. Some people were injected in the arm. Some were injected in the shoulder. Some were injected in the back. I suspect it was absolute pandemonium. And Jones ordered the deaths of the children first. And once you kill my child, what do I have to live for? Or once you kill my mother or my father or my sister, and that's all I have, what am I living for? So I think a lot of people gave up when they saw what was happening around them that day.

It was on the twenty-first, when they said, "Everybody's gone," that I realized that Ollie was dead. Babies, children, women, everybody's dead. If everybody's gone, she's gone. That's when I broke down on the balcony. Teena and Joan held me up and said, "It's gonna be okay, Eugene. We're gonna make it through this." I was destroyed. First I felt guilt, then unbridled rage. That rage didn't leave for years.

Now we're up to the twenty-second of November, and the GDF have lightened up a bit, but they haven't lightened up on me. "You let this white man kill your family? You followed this white man here? The fuck's wrong with you?" There is no answer to that. They're looking at us like, "You fucking idiots. What's wrong with you?" I was mad. They were mad. They had lost Guyanese citizens. I had lost my family. How do you weigh that?

So they finally started lightening up. The first three days were hell. If you started falling asleep, they'd rap their AKs just to keep you awake. They figured, "If we tire them down, they'll tell us everything we want to know." But we didn't know anything, and they finally understood that. They started lightening up on everyone after a week or so but the GPF, the Guyana Police Force, hadn't lightened up yet. But after a couple weeks we were running out of food and had to shop for supplies, which meant we had to go to an open-air market.

So we get in the back of the Bedford. We've got the GDF with us, guards and whatnot, and people in the market are pointing at us and yelling, "Yankee go home! Yankee go home!" They recognize the truck, and believe me, even when you're in a Black country and you're a Black person but you're from the States, you still stand out like a white person. They can tell by your clothes and by your demeanor, even if you carry yourself with humility. There were things that were valuable to them, that were everyday items for us, like Fruit of the Loom. They paid a premium price for Fruit of the Loom underwear. "Cotton underwear? Yes. How much do you want?"

We get our food supplies, and we get back. It's a bit distressing to be called a murderer. That wears on you. Now we're into our third or fourth week, and they're allowing us to get away from the house and come back. Not totally unsupervised, but less supervision. We're getting the news reports from the States, and people are coming into the airports. Relatives of people who died in Jonestown are coming into the Georgetown airport with weapons. "My mother or father or sister or brother died. How come yours didn't?" These are relatives that are coming into the airport and getting stopped. And we're under guard again, because now it's Americans wanting to kill us. The Guyanese hate us, and the Americans want to kill us, and the whole world thinks we're nuts.

I contact the Cuban embassy, friend of a friend, and say, "Hey, I can't go back to the States. There's no way I can go back." She says, "Well, you can't come to Cuba either, at least not for another year or so. You gotta figure it out. Maybe even two more years." It wasn't that Cuba didn't want us, but they couldn't take the political fallout from this. And Russia says, "Yeah, we'll take you in a little bit, but you're gonna be under heavy observation. You're not gonna be anywhere alone. We don't trust you either." I didn't quite understand what their take was.

Now it's like we can't grieve, because we haven't seen any bodies, and everybody's assuming that many of the bodies still haven't been identified. It turned out they didn't even start identifying the bodies until a month later, and even then a full third of them, including my son Martin, ended up being buried unidentified. They're getting ready to come back to the US, but to Dover Air Force Base on the East Coast. They tried to refrigerate them but failed. Then they shipped them by truck out to the West Coast, and they couldn't find any place to bury them. There was difficulty finding a cemetery that would accept more than four hundred unclaimed and unidentified dead. Most cemeteries in the Bay Area refused to have anything to do with them, until finally Evergreen Cemetery in Oakland agreed.

People were coming into the country all the time and, since we were now allowed some free rein, we could pick up stories from newspapers. *Time* magazine has a picture of the vat of cyanide on the cover. We hear about that, and then *Time* is somehow able to access letters from people who were under duress, some of whom died on November 18, some still alive. Unless you know the person or the circumstance, the letters are way out of context. It's like, "I'm writing this letter, but I'm trying to live at the same time. I'm trying to tell you something, but I can't tell you. Can you please read between these lines?" Americans aren't reading between the lines. America is reading the lines as they were written and cannot perceive anything else outside of that.

So it starts getting stressful at the house at Lamaha Gardens. We always had alcohol in the house. Alcohol was used as bribery to give to officials in the Guyanese administration, the ministry of this, secretary of that. "Oh, here. Take a bottle of this Johnny Walker. Tell me how you like it." The Guyanese loved tube socks, for some reason, and Fruit of the Loom underwear. We had a little bit of American currency. If you sold it on the black market the exchange rate was four or five to one, because you didn't have to declare it. I met up with some girls who lived across the street from the prison in Georgetown and sold them some currency.

I never was much of a drinker. That just wasn't my thing. But I was smoking probably two packs of cigarettes a day. On a bad day, I smoked three packs. I found some pot—finally, a release. We're out there smoking a joint, Beau, Lee Ingram, and myself, between Lamaha Gardens and the GDF base across the street. The joint was rolled in butcher paper, because you couldn't find ZigZag paper in Guyana. We're sitting out there in the grass, looking up at the sky, because there's nothing else to look at. The stars look like they're right in front of your face. It's just an hour or so of complete peace. An alternate universe, for that brief hour.

This is the second week after the incident, the end of November. We'd been going through all this shit. Those who drank had drunk up as much alcohol as they possibly could. There was a lot of alcohol, because there were a lot of people to bribe. That's when people start leaving. That's when they start saying, "Okay, it's your time to go." So people are leaving the house. Things have finally been worked out with the State Department. They're willing to accept us back into the US.

At Lamaha Gardens, we didn't run into any contingent of American officials. Guyana was still a socialist country, and they weren't going to let Americans run wild. They let the State Department and the US military into Jonestown, and the FBI could begin its preliminary inquiry out of the US Embassy, but they didn't give them access to us at Lamaha Gardens. But once we left and got to the airport, we were assigned a US air marshal. Their responsibility was to make sure nobody harmed us. But they made it quite clear: "We don't give a shit about you." This was our first contact with Americans. They just glared at us. Basically, "You're fucking nuts. You just haven't been committed yet. When we get you back to the US, you're going to an insane asylum." They didn't say that, but that was how they treated us.

I left Guyana on the twenty-ninth of December. The flight was something like six hours, straight from Georgetown to JFK. It was a commercial flight, but it was like a prison flight. It seems like there were regular people on there, but they were way up front, and we were a large contingent and way in the back, and there was a buffer zone. There were sky marshals in front of us, behind us, and on the side. We were encased by sky marshals. And the feeling was that they didn't really give a shit about us. It was their job just to get us to the US, and if something happened in the meantime, well, it'll just happen. It was like being at Lamaha Gardens that first morning, with the Guyanese Defence Force outside and all their guns pointing in rather than out. It was the next version of that, except now it's US sky marshals, and they were packing heavy. As far as they were concerned we were brainwashed maniacs, and any of us at any time could go off. And they wanted to minimize that threat without bringing down the plane, because they had read FBI files that mentioned my name, Stephan's name, Jimmy Jr.'s name, claiming we had been instructed to bring that plane down without any survivors.

The FBI had been told the reason we weren't in Jonestown on November 18 was that we were Jones's avenging angels. So when the FBI interrogator asked if I had heard of angels, I said, "No." I had been called an angel, in a bad way, and there was no way I was going to admit to that. At the same time, they had no compassion about us losing our family and friends. I remember describing it to someone. I said, "You go to sleep one night, on the couch in the front room. Your wife is in the bedroom. Your child is in the other bedroom. You wake up the next morning. Your child is dead. Your wife is dead. You go outside. Everybody on your block is dead. There's no buses. There's no traffic. You go down to the store. Everybody in the store is dead. Everybody's dead at the gas station." My whole life stopped that day. There's no recovery from that. There's no justification for that. There's no way to explain it. And people kept asking, "Explain it. Explain it. Explain it." I can't. And that created even more anger. "You're holding back. You're not telling us what we want to know." But I can't tell you what I don't know.

The overnight flight to JFK on December 29 was stressful because, on one hand, I'm coming back to the US after we'd all been forced to renounce our citizenship. The Temple had confiscated our passports as soon as we first arrived in Georgetown. So none of us had passports. But when the State Department went into Jonestown, they found all of our passports, amazingly. So before we got on, they handed us all back our passports, but then they confiscated them again when we got to New York. And the United States government charged me anyway for the next flight, from New York to LA, which was three hundred and some-odd dollars in those days. They said, "We'll pay for your flight, but you owe us." Later, in 1999, when I applied for a new passport, I had to pay them back for that fucking flight.

I'm coming back to the United States, knowing that I'm hated. I'm hated by my wife's family. My own family doesn't really know where I am. And I'm despised. We survivors are despised by people we don't even know, because of an incident that we didn't take part in. We didn't commit murder, but we were called murderers, child killers, lunatics, brainwashed, cultists. There were still people at the Temple in San Francisco and LA, still clearing out all the belongings. Attorneys were coming in claiming property, looking for all the assets of Peoples Temple: all the foreign bank accounts, the Social Security and child welfare checks that were being sent for people that were there, all the governmental checks that were being sent to support Jonestown, roughly $36,000 a month. All that was going on, and it was coming out in the news, but with no explanation and no context. We were innocent, but we were still being thrown to the wolves, guilty by association.

What made it so difficult to defend against was, "Hey, you were there. Why didn't you do anything?" Well, you're 250 miles from civilization. You're in this jungle. You're coming from a city environment. Even if you were a hunter-gatherer, or an outdoorsman or survivalist, it was a difficult situation to be in. And you didn't know who your friends were, even though you had known these people for years. Once you were there, your friendships were compromised by dedication or by "I'm here for the cause, I'm here for Peoples Temple, I'm here for Jim Jones, I'm here for socialism. Friendships don't really mean anything to me now." And friendships changed drastically, because the level of paranoia was so high.

When we got to JFK it was twenty-three degrees and I had on my jungle stuff, but I wasn't allowed to get to my checked luggage. They offloaded the plane, then they offloaded us. And they just let us sit there and freeze. I'm wearing khaki pants with a safari jacket, but real light. And at JFK they used to have these hallways that had PlexiGlas windows. People on the other side were just bang, bang, bang, bang, bang, bang, banging on it, banging and screaming. There were so many people screaming and banging, I could not distinguish what they were saying. It was just a mob. They were people who were concerned, who were afraid, who were mad, who felt that these people had been cheated out of their lives, and they wanted to make the point that they were upset with us: "Although you survived, we're not happy about that. All those people were killed, some murdered, some committed suicide, we're not happy about that either. But we really don't like you guys, because you survived." As far as I know, they were not friends or family members of people who had died at Jonestown. But they were in unison in terms of their dislike for us as returning survivors. It was a mob mentality, basically. This was only about six weeks after the incident. Nerves were still raw. The stories about abuse and punishment were still coming out. Stories about starvation and torture and cruelty. There were also other people coming out of the woodwork who weren't there, who said they had been abused, there had been scare tactics, they had been threatened. It was all in the air. So I get it. It was just that they were reacting to the wrong people.

Then we got into the terminal, and they escorted us through customs. They confiscated our passports. Then the questioning started: "What's your name? Where were you born? What's your mother's name? What's your father's name? What cottage did you live in? How long have you been involved in the Temple? Did you kill anybody?" I was like, "No." It was a whole series of questions through different entities: CIA, FBI, State Department. Most of the questions had to do with who lived in what hut, who were Jones's bodyguards, was I on the Planning Commission. They all just centered around that. They didn't care about, "Who did you lose? Are you okay? Do you want to see a doctor?" None of that. And they started going through our luggage. They squeezed out the toothpaste. They shook out the mouthwash. They went through everything. The Secret Service was there; I don't know why. They didn't say anything. I'm saying the same thing I said in Guyana: "I don't know. I want an attorney." They said, "Okay," then came back five minutes later with this Italian guy. His shoes cost more than everything I had on and everything in my luggage and everything I had left. Just his shoes. He was walking around with two grand on his back. I said, "No, I don't want him."

Then they handed me a subpoena to appear in front of the Ninth Circuit Court. "On this date in January, you have to be in San Francisco." We're still not on our own yet; we've still got guards. They wanted to verify that we got on that airplane. It was going to fly from JFK to LA, then to San Francisco, because there were members getting off in LA and members getting off in San Francisco. There was no transferring of flights. They did not trust us that far. After they were done interrogating us, they put me and Herbert Newell in the Howard Johnson's motel by JFK overnight. I have a fifty-dollar bill in the bottom of my white Converse high-top tennis shoes, beneath the innersole, that I've been saving forever. It's all the money I have in the world. I bring it out, it has holes in it, but it's still spendable. I use that to buy us breakfast. We had left Georgetown on the twenty-ninth and landed at JFK on the thirtieth. On the morning of the thirty-first, New Year's Eve, some alphabet agency picked me and Herbert up at the Howard Johnson's, escorted us to JFK, and verified that we boarded the plane.

They asked us where we were going. I said San Francisco, and Herbert said Los Angeles. And Herbert and I are talking, and I say, "Hey Herbert, man. Look, dude, when you get home, don't say nothing about this. Don't tell nobody that this happened. Don't let nobody know who you are. Don't let nobody know where you've been. Don't tell nobody where you're going. This is not gonna end well for us. Don't talk to nobody about this, because we're marked. They've already seen pictures of us. Hopefully we can blend into society, but I don't think so."

Then I said, "Who's picking you up?"

He said, "Jackie's picking me up."

And I said, "Can I get a ride out to Compton?"

He said, "Yeah."

I said, "I told 'em I'm going to San Francisco, but I'm getting off."

So I left my shit, just left. Got off the plane. I had bags, but I just left them. Got off the plane. Had whatever I could carry, what I brought on the plane with me, but my luggage was underneath. I don't know what happened to it.

So we're outside waiting, and Jackie pulls up. I knew Jackie. "Hey, Jackie. How you doing?"

And she's like, "Hey, Eugene. I wasn't expecting you."

I said, "You mind dropping me off in Compton?"

She said, "Sure."

I was going to Compton because I had made contact with a man there named J. W. Osborne. Because my mom had told me, "If you ever get in trouble, you contact J. W. He'll be there." When Jackie dropped me at his house J. W. was at work, but I had spoken to his wife, Utte. Really beautiful woman, redhead, just gorgeous sister. Jackie let me out, and I walked up to the door and knocked on it. And Utte said, "Who is it?"

I said, "It's Butch."

And through the door she said, "I love you."

And I hadn't heard that in I don't know how long. And she let me in the house, and she sat me down. She said, "Baby, I know you've gone through a lot. J. W.'s at work. I'll let him know you're here."

CHAPTER 2
Nothing Left to Lose

I grew up in Fresno. I was eight when the Watts riot happened, and ten when the Detroit riot happened. I saw the riots on TV. Mom said, "I'm glad we're not in LA or Detroit." Those things are what molded me, because finally somebody was fighting for what they fucking believed in. I was going to the Adventist Academy. The car picked me up every morning at 7:30 and dropped me off at school, and at 3:30 the car was waiting for me at the front gate to take me home. Farmworkers lived next door and across the street, but I was insulated from all that. I was protected. All I knew from what I was seeing on TV was that Black people in LA and Detroit were fighting for something they believed in, and they weren't getting treated right. I was getting treated right, so I didn't have that fight. But at fifteen I did, because I was no longer in private school. There was no longer a car picking me up and dropping me off. I was going to a mostly white public high school in Fresno.

I was too young for Vietnam. But in 1974, when I was seventeen, just before I went to San Francisco, a recruiter stopped me on my bike and said, "How old are you?"

I said, "I'm seventeen."

"Have you registered yet?"

"No. I haven't registered yet."

"We want to make sure we see you in the military," he said.

I knew right then: "Fuck you, I'm not joining that shit."

At seventeen I was still gaining, still finding out. But at twenty-two, when I was back in Fresno after Jonestown and after eight months in Compton, I had lost everything. If they had asked me then, I would've joined. But I knew they wouldn't ask me, because of my record. There was no way they were going to let me in the military. That was a pipe dream. I had nothing. Everything was lost; I had nothing left to lose. At eighteen in 1975, I could almost have been the last American soldier to die in Vietnam. At twenty-two, in 1979, I wouldn't have minded, because I had lost all my fear. I didn't care about being shot, I didn't care about having a wreck. I didn't care about driving off a cliff. I didn't care about being beaten. I had no fear, and a Black man in America with no fear is a very dangerous thing. I think our government recognized that in some of us, which is why we were followed for years after the fact. It's why we were observed and monitored: because we don't have any fear.

At some point you shut down. But then, when you're given an opportunity to speak out about what you've lived through and not be ostracized or penalized for it, you take that, because now you can get it off your chest. It's not so much a "Screw you," but more like, "This is my truth."

This book has been a long time coming. I pitched it to multiple publishers and multiple authors, and multiple folks in the African American community, and nobody would touch it. So I didn't build up an animosity behind it, but I did build up an attitude of "Your loss." It's about me, but it's your history too. And you wonder why people join groups like Peoples Temple. This is why: Because they're asking for help, and you're in a position to give it, and you won't even offer it. It's different if you're not in a position, and you say, "Hey there's nothing I can do for you." But if you're already doing for yourself what I'm asking you to do for me, and you refuse to do it for me, I'm going to be disappointed and disgusted.

So now I'm doing it myself, telling my story. This book is my truth.

After Jonestown I came back. Jonestown had been a massive, tragic failure. But I was coming back into the same American society that I had left and said I'd never come back to. But coming back to the US gave me priorities. And once you set priorities, things become either very significant or insignificant. The most significant thing was survival. Not living, not having fun, not having a great time. Just basic survival. Food in mouth, clothes on back, shoes on feet, roof over head. Survival. Not fancy survival; bare minimum survival. Because all I had was the fifty dollars I came back with, and I broke that to buy breakfast for Herbert Newell and myself at the Howard Johnson near JFK Airport. So it was about survival and coming into an environment with my mother's best friend, J. W. Osborne, in Compton. And trying not to scare his family, and trying not to influence the children with the dynamics of what I've gone through.

And having gone out into the world, and having seen the US from afar, having lived afar then come back, and now I'm no longer seeing it from afar, I'm experiencing it, I had a choice to either get mad, or get bitter, or get even. I was going to be sad regardless. I was going to be remorseful regardless. But those three items—getting mad, bitter, or even—I could deal with. I wasn't going to be bitter, because once you're bitter, even when things correct themselves, it doesn't matter because you're bitter. Getting mad doesn't serve me because, if I do, I'm going to be perceived as an angry Black man.

So: How do you get even? You go out and you succeed. My success was different from other survivors, those who had been raised in Peoples Temple. They had never seen anything else. They hadn't been on the outside. They had only been on the inside. That's neither good nor bad nor indifferent. It just is. Their success was to get back, get a job, create a business, make a family, have a future generation to carry on not the name, but something better than the name. Jimmy—Jim Jones Jr.—didn't change his name. Some people changed their names when they got back. Jimmy didn't. My father didn't wear shining armor either, but I didn't have his name. So I could always say I didn't know him. Jimmy Jr. doesn't have that luxury. And he could have changed his name, but he chose not to. What he did choose to do was to create a family and let the name carry forward without the tragedy. That makes sense for him. Stephan Jones created a family. The majority of them created families.

But I could not do that, because I wasn't raised in that environment. The environment I was raised in said that I had failed, and that there was no coming back. I had failed my wife and child and extended family. I had lost all of that. The Jones boys and others came back to extended families and support systems. I didn't have those. Things might have been different, had I had a support system. But I'm not blaming that on anybody; that's just the way it was.

What I'm saying is that when you come back and there's a support system that says, "We love you," like J. W. Osborne's wife Utte said to me when I first got back, it gives you hope to change, to do more. But what it didn't do was make me want to raise a family. I don't want a family anymore. I'm not interested in raising children. I will assist in raising children, I will help children who are in need, I will read to them, I will nurture them, I will give them the best unbiased advice that I can. What I will not do is try to create a certain mindset for them. I think that's wrong, because that's what happened in Peoples Temple. A lot of children in the Temple had a mindset that they were socialist revolutionaries. But how can you know what that means when you're only eight years old? But what Americans don't understand, that people in most countries understand that have had strife and upheaval, is that children and women start the revolution. Men fight it. And the reason women and children start the revolution is that women are the first ones affected. So their first thing is, "I need to protect my child." That's a revolt. And children aren't born with fear; they learn fear. If you get them to a certain point without that fear, they will die for what they believe in. It's like the Cultural Revolution in China. And if you look at revolutions around the world, you see children. Because they see what their mothers are going through to protect them. So men fight the revolution, but it's women and children that start it. I knew inside of me that if I raised a boy, he was going to be angry. There was no way around that, because I would set him up with so many mechanisms to protect himself that he would be angry. If I had a girl, I'd be so protective of her that she'd be angry as well. I can't lose again. So that was my reasoning, as wild and as crazy as it might seem. For me, it was logical.

I had lost my wife and child and my mother, and every friend I'd made in the last five or six years. Every girlfriend, ex-girlfriend, broken relationship, created relationship. People I'd argued with, people I'd fought with, people I'd made friends with, people I'd made enemies with, people I didn't respect, people I hated, people I loved, people I was infatuated with. Every dynamic you can think of was gone from my life, in one day.

Afterward I sought out friends to a certain extent, but when I was first in LA and roaming around, former Temple members would run when they saw me. That hurt. Because I never harmed you, and I never meant you any harm, and all I did was be lucky enough to not be part of a tragic situation, and you treat me as an aggressor. And now they had found Jesus, or they had found So-and-so, but they couldn't forgive me. But I'm not the one who did the murdering; I only went there. So there's nothing to forgive me for. And the people who knew who I was and what I had been through handled me with kid gloves, because of all the media going on. And the media went on for a couple years after Jonestown, into the eighties: "These are cultists, they're this, they're that." In March 1979, Mike Prokes, who had escaped Jonestown through the jungle with the Carter brothers, committed suicide. A couple of high-profile former members got shot. One former member shot two students in an LA schoolyard, then shot himself. Other members went to jail. And it was all a feeding frenzy for the news media to pick up on. "Because of that, they did this." All these what-ifs, or what could have happened, or why didn't they do this. But you can't look at individuals like that. I mean, you can, and people do. But we should give individuals, human beings, more credit than one situation dictating who they are for the rest of their life.

It was a tragic situation and everything, but it was a few hours of extreme violence, preceded by moments of tranquility and peace. But we're all judged by that moment: November 18, 1978. That twenty-four fucking hours is the bane of my life. That fucking moment. It's a nightmare that you never wake up from. It's a bad dream that you never quit dreaming. It's a bad moment that keeps repeating itself. It's Dante's hell, forty years later. Because no matter how long I live, no matter what magnanimous things I have done or might do, I'm always going to be associated with that moment.

I was tasked with being a survivor. A survivor had a specific responsibility, as I saw it. My first responsibility as a survivor, when I came back, was not to embarrass my mother or my wife or my child, and to set an example that can't be questioned. In other words, if I come back and I'm this thug, I justify the mistreatment of survivors based on me being a thug. Or being a jerk. I knew that when I came back, I had to be squeaky clean. Coming back, I had a target on my back: "If you do fuck up, we're gonna fuck you up. Because we don't want you walking around free anyway." They made that pretty obvious before we left Guyana: "We don't want you back in the US." And Guyana made it clear too: "We don't want you here either." But there was nowhere else for me to go.

No, I had to continue living. And I couldn't take myself out, at least not purposely. Now, going 140 miles an hour in an Alfa Romeo or on a motorcycle, if I get killed, oh well. It's like, "Oh, it was an accident." If I get shot, "Oh well, it's an accident, I didn't do it on purpose." It's the same as with some combat veterans. That's why I didn't have an issue when I worked at Standard Oil in the eighties, because those guys were all ex-military. They'd say, "Where'd you fight at?" I said, "I fought in Fresno. My combat boots were Converse." They'd laugh. I'd say, "I'm serious. My combat boots were Converse. At least you had combat boots." That's how I felt then, that's how I feel now. But I'm okay now. I don't have the anger that I once had.

They say you mellow with age. You don't. You become more calculated with age. And you understand when and how to vent your anger, rather than irrationally acting out. You don't mellow with age; you educate yourself with age on how to control your anger and how best to use it, either to motivate yourself to do something, or to do something you don't want to do. You get angry by saying, "Fuck it, let me get this out of the way. I'm tired of looking at it," and you deal with it. That's how I've done it.

So in early 1979 I was just sitting there, at J. W. Osborne's house in Compton, trying to decompress, because I'd been under fucking stress for months. And it's like I didn't know how to be sensitive, or how to hug anybody, because I had been on guard. If it wasn't the Guyanese soldiers, it was the Guyanese detective, or the FBI, or some other alphabet agency.

Chuck Beikman had been arrested in connection with the murders of Sharon, Liane, Christa, and Martin Amos. And it was like, "Damn, I worked with this guy." But in his defense, Chuck Beikman had come out of Appalachia, literally out of a shack with no plumbing, not a pot to piss in or a window to throw it out. And Jim Jones gave him a name. Jones made him somebody we should respect. Chuck had skills that we needed in the cause. People would say, "He's just poor white trash," but this was a man who had lied to get into the Marines early because he just wanted to get away. And then some kind of way he got in touch with Jones, like a lot of people who were just walking around San Francisco saying, "Whoa. I'll go listen to you. What you talking about?" And Chuck Beikman felt he owed Jim Jones: "I owe you. Whatever you say do, I'll do." And he would have killed those four, if Jones had asked him to. But the fact is that he didn't. He was eventually charged with the attempted murder of Stephanie Jones, the only one to survive the carnage in the Lamaha Gardens bathroom, and he spent five years in a Guyanese jail for the crime. But he didn't kill anyone.

But in early 1979 no one knew anything yet, other than that Chuck had been arrested. And all this is going on in my head, sitting there in J. W.'s house in Compton. Nobody wants to say they know a murderer. And nobody wants to defend a murderer. But it was more nuanced than that. And so when Utte said she loved me, it hit me hard. I hadn't seen her in years, but I hadn't been told that in a long time. I had told her I was coming back. I just didn't know what day. And it was hard calling from Guyana to the US, because the phone lines were poor and they were all monitored. You'd hear clicks and shit in the background.

So I get there, and I see J. W.'s daughter, Lisa. "Hey Butch, how you doing?" And she doesn't really know what's going on. Utte and Lisa told the foster children, "This is Butch. He's gonna be staying here a while." It was a duplex, and Utte's son Larry was up front with his wife, Bernadette, who happened to be from Georgetown, Guyana. She was a manager at a McDonald's, and Larry worked at UCLA. He'd been a medic in Vietnam. Everybody was happy to see me, but they were like, "Yeah, we're happy to see you, but where's your head?"

So J. W. gets in that night, and he says, "Ah. Glad you're back okay. Need you to drive." And I hadn't driven in over a year because I was in Jonestown, in the bush. But I still had my driver's license. I hadn't turned in my driver's license or my Social Security card. So we get in this car. It's a 1978 Fleetwood Brougham, and we're driving through LA. We go to visit family friends who had known my mother, and who had known me as a kid. Alex and his sons, Ricky and I forget the younger son's name, and his daughter. And J. W.'s getting rip-roaring drunk. And I said, "Hey, look, I want to get home before the shooting starts. I don't need that in my life right now. Look, we need to get home. I don't want to be in this shooting in LA." This is New Year's Eve, my very first night there. And I had arrived back in the United States only the day before.

So we're talking, drinking a little bit. And finally I say, "We gotta go. It's getting late. It's getting towards midnight. It's New Year's Eve." And we're driving back, and as we pull into the driveway, it has an easement into the house next door, and there's a guy standing in the driveway with a rifle. And I'm looking at him, and he's firing. And as he's firing, the gun is lowering. Just as it reaches the roof line, I push J. W. down and I punch it. I try to run the guy over. I hit the garage door opener. The door gets as high as the hood of the car, and then we go through it. The only thing stopping the car was the back wall. I crawl out. J. W.'s still in there, kind of drunk. There were no airbags in those days, but the seat belts would snag you. So I crawl out of the garage and up to the patio door. I say, "Utte, let me in. Give me the guns. Give me the guns." Because I knew J. W. always had a gun, but I didn't think he had one in the car that night.

So she hands me a gun out. By the time I get back into the garage, J. W.'s out of the car. The guy has a rifle, and J. W. is waving a .38 in his face: "The hell you doing? Blah, blah, blah." He's screaming. I say, "Stop it, J. W. Don't say nothing else." The police never showed. Nobody called the police. But the next day I wrote out what happened, so J. W. ended up suing the neighbor. I don't know what the result of that was, but I had to write that. I had been back in the United States for forty-eight hours, and I already had an auto accident and tried to run somebody over, and the man I'm staying with was trying to shoot his neighbor.

So I wake up the next morning and remember that I just wrecked J. W.'s brand-new Cadillac. I'm feeling terrible. He says, "Don't worry about it." J. W. always got his Cadillacs from the Cadillac factory in Detroit. When his car was delivered, it was totally customized for him. He used to drink so much that he specified for the jets for the windshield wipers to come inside the car. When he pressed the wiper fluid, it would spray out gin beneath the dashboard. He didn't use the wiper fluid for the wipers. He put his gin in there, so he could drink on the road. But I felt really bad. Everybody said, "Don't worry about it. Don't worry about it. Don't worry about it." But I'm thinking to myself, "They think I'm crazy. I know they think that." But the guy had a rifle, and he was lowering it.

The next day, which must have been a weekend day because I don't think he went to work—I got there on a Friday—I said, "I'm gonna apologize." He says, "Don't worry about it." Then I went into the back porch, and I put on the Dramatics, I think "In the Rain" or something, songs I used to listen to. And then I said, "I gotta get a job." And he kept asking me, "So tell me about your mother. Tell me about Mattie," because they were best friends. So I said, "I can't tell you nothing. I hadn't seen her in months." And before the few months I did see her in Jonestown, I hadn't seen her in over a year. He got really mad at me for not knowing about my mom, because she was his best friend. He didn't get vengeful. He was just like, "Okay, if you don't want to talk about it, you ain't gotta fucking talk about it."

"It's not that I don't want to talk about it," I told him. "I have nothing to tell you."

"Well, what happened?"

"I don't know." That recurring phrase: "I don't know."

I figured he got drunk because I was there. Later on in the week Utte told me, "He quit drinking when he was worried about you. Once he found out you were alive, he started drinking again." I said, "Okay. Well, I'll take him for a ride if he gets kinda rowdy." He'd cuss Utte out and tell Lisa, "You're not my daughter. My daughter ain't got no nose like that." But she was his daughter. And he was just really mean and vengeful. When he got drunk it was like, "What can I say to hurt you?" But he never would do it to me. He only abused them. And I said, "Come on, let's go. You don't have to stay here. Let's go." I'd always take him out of the house, and they would thank me for it. But it wore on me.

After about four days he got me a job, working with Steve at Steve's Carwash on Compton Boulevard. So I was working there a couple weeks, getting tips and whatnot. And I'm hearing all this stuff coming across the news about Jonestown, how some of the survivors came back: Be careful of them, be watchful of them, be aware of them. And I'd be in LA, or I might go down to Pico Boulevard or Alvarado, just to get away, just to walk around or to see the old LA Temple, and I'd see old members, and they'd see me and run, because I was out of place. "You're the last person I expected to fucking see." That hurt, knowing that people would see me and run. I wasn't something to be very proud of.

Utte's daughter-in-law from Guyana, Bernadette, knew that I wasn't really happy working at the car wash, so she offered me a job at McDonald's. But I only lasted two days there, because I couldn't handle all the beeping. If it beeps twice, take the fries out. If it beeps once, your Big Mac is done. It was all these commands by beeps. I couldn't take it. Gardena, the town next to Compton, had a business district with a lot of industrial shops. In those days, if you were willing to walk for a couple hours, you could get a job. So I walked up and down that boulevard filling out applications. Within a couple days I got a call from the 4-Day Tire Store, offering me a job. Changing tires, doing rotations, fixing flats, finding specialized tires. Anything to do with a tire.

A few weeks after I started at 4-Day, the FBI showed up there looking for me. I'm off work that day, or I had already left, or something. So they leave a card. I come in the next day and my boss says, "Eugene, the FBI was here, said they're looking for you."

"No, it must be my brother," I told him. "It couldn't have been me."

"Well, they said they just wanted to talk to you." Here's a strange slant or odd thing: Like me, my supervisor at 4-Day Tire was adopted. Not that it means anything, but it's just the circles of people you meet in life. Being a fellow adoptee, he understood extended family and all that kind of stuff. And he was a white guy.

About the feds, you have to ask: Why were they mad at Jim Jones? They were mad at Jim Jones because of his protector and mentor in Guyana, the socialist prime minister, Forbes Burnham. Shell Oil Company was there in Guyana, and the US government did not want a communist state, so to speak, that close to the US border. So Forbes Burnham was somebody to be dealt with. He was given ten million dollars not to court the Russians. What did he do? He took the ten million, courted the Russians anyway, and nationalized all the commercial interests in the country, including Shell Oil. And then the Russians came in and started building a power plant. So, with that being the case, then you got this guy, Jones, down there on his so-called agricultural mission, because he wants to escape capitalism, because he's a socialist. "We really hate you now. We didn't like you in the first place, and now we hate you." Who knows what they thought about it, actually. They might have thought it was a satellite for the Russians. Who knows? In any case, it put us survivors in the crosshairs. Because, as you know, America doesn't like socialists close to its border.

So the feds followed me. They harassed me at JFK. Secret Service was there at JFK; I couldn't figure that one out. The State Department was there; I couldn't figure that one out. The CIA was there, and the FBI, and I guess other alphabet agencies that weren't named were there. Everybody had their questions: "We want you to answer everything about everybody, because we know you know." When I said, "No, no, no, no, no," they said, "Okay, well, here's your subpoena. You're subpoenaed to appear in court in San Francisco."

So I get home from the tire store to J. W.'s house in Compton, and I call the FBI, Special Agent So-and-so. I said, "This is Eugene Smith, I hear you're lookin' for me."

"Oh yeah, we came by your job."

"Why'd you do that?"

"Well, we wanted to get your attention." Quote. "We wanted to get your attention."

"Okay, you got my attention. What do you want?"

"Well, we want to get a handwriting analysis so that, if a politician or political figure is threatened in the future, we can automatically X you out, because we already have a sample of your handwriting."

"Okay, so when you want to do that?"

"Well, tomorrow's okay."

"Fine. Well, you obviously know where I stay, since you know where I work."

Two agents show up the next day. I tell J. W. He goes to work. I tell Utte, "Hey, the FBI are coming by. I don't really know what this is about." They come by. They sit in the living room. And I'm fucking furious, because I didn't want to bring anybody else into my shit. This is my world, this *I Spy* shit. This is my involvement, not the family's. So they talk to me for a few minutes. "Okay, would you go ahead and write the following?" They give me some kind of lectern. I do the handwriting sample. They say, "Thank you very much. We'll be in contact if anything happens in the future." I say, "Okay, nice to see you. Leave." And they leave.

I'm apologetic to the family. "Oh, no, don't worry about it, Butch. It's okay."

"I didn't want you guys to be involved in this," I say. "I didn't want your address involved in this or anything."

"Don't worry about it," they keep assuring me.

But soon after that, I left for Fresno by virtue of invite. I remember calling back and asking, "Did the FBI ever come back to the house again and harass you guys?" J. W. said no, nothing ever happened after that. I said, "I'm grateful. I didn't want you guys to be harassed or anything."

But I suspect the phones in Compton were tapped for a long time. I had to get out of Compton. The FBI were coming to the house. That's too comfortable for them, and too uncomfortable for me. But I never knowingly heard from the FBI again. I know that sounds funny, to say *not knowingly*. Alphabet agencies communicate in different ways. Either it's a very subtle message, or it's a very overt message. Never is it just a regular message. It's either very subtle, so only you know about it, or it's very overt, so the world knows about it. There's nothing in between, like a phone call: "Hey, we're watching you this week."

I ended up living for eight months in Compton, with J. W. Osborne and his family, before I decided I had to leave. That first month, January, I had to go up to San Francisco for my court date. It was different, being there and not being able to go to the Temple. All the communes were gone. My friends that let me stay with them, Steve McIntosh and Pumpkin, lived on Divisidero. I stayed the night with them, went to court the next day, and left the next evening.

Steve and Pumpkin asked me: "Are you okay?"

"Yeah, I'm all right," I told them.

And they said, "Don't worry about it. You didn't do anything wrong."

I could tell that Steve and Pumpkin could tell that I had changed from the person I had been before I left. I didn't divulge anything to them other than "They killed Ollie and they killed my baby," because I didn't want them to have to lie on my behalf.

My hearing lasted a few hours. They asked me about the location of certain huts at Jonestown. "I don't know nothin'," I told them. They never asked me about who I lost, or whether I was hurting. I was really mad about that. Even now, I'm really fucking mad about that. To them, my loss was an incidental loss. The message was, "You're expendable too. You just happened not to be there that day, but it would have been no loss if you had been." By the time I got back to LA, I was flaming.

I go back to work at the 4-Day Tire Store, and J. W. is still a fucking drunk. He liked gin and Schlitz beer, from Milwaukee. I cared for Utte and for J. W.'s daughter Lisa, and for their three children. But the foster kids are just being kids, and I'm way beyond my years—I'm twenty-one but it's like I'm fifty. And eventually I'm just like, "I gotta go." I had never really liked LA anyway, and I got tired of being a babysitter for this guy. It just wore on me, until it came to a head. There wasn't any one incident; it was dozens of incidents that accumulated. I was grateful, so I thought the best thing to do was for me to leave. I was fed up with J. W., which gave me justification for my decision. I was tired of having to drive him around drunk. Not that this means anything, but he was a weekend drunk. Friday night to Sunday night. You can deal with a happy drunk. It's the mean ones that make you hate alcohol. He was verbally mean. So I made the escape, again, to my mother's friend Mary

Cromer in Fresno, where I had grown up. "Hey, if you have an issue, call Mary Cromer."

Mary was part Mexican and part German. My mother and Mary were friends from before the Temple, and Mary still believed in Jim Jones. She thought he had been set up by the CIA. The Cromers sold clothes from Gottschalks department store. They'd take orders, and they had a connection inside the store who took a cut. Shirts, coats, slacks, double knit. A lot of my own clothes growing up came from Gottschalks by way of the Cromers.

"Come on down," Mary said to me when I called. "Anita will pick you up at the bus station." Their place was just like I remembered, out in the country, with an olive orchard off to the side. There was a small airport nearby, Chandler Executive Airport. It took me about ten minutes to get into the city, to a neighborhood. I was just far enough out in the country so I was comfortable, but close enough that I had access. Initially I lived in the main house, but thirty or forty feet from the back door was a disused water tower. It had been empty for who knows how long. I mentioned that I would like to remove the holding tank and move up there, and it took Mary only about a week to have it renovated. So I had a bedroom that was like forty feet in the air. I was happy, because it allowed me the privacy that I needed.

CHAPTER 3

Choosing to Engage

I was born in Detroit, Michigan, on July 29, 1957. A few days after I was born, I was adopted by a middle-aged woman named Mattie Battle. The way this came about was that I was the second child out of wedlock of my biological mother, Lillian Joyce Smith. She was a member of New Bethel Baptist Church, where Rev. C. L. Franklin, Aretha Franklin's father, was the minister. Because I was her second child out of wedlock, I got the golden straw to be adopted out. My grandmother was friends with my adoptive mother, and the decision was made that this child had to be adopted out.

My father had brought his fiancée and my two half-sisters out to Detroit in 1957 to introduce them to Mattie, my adoptive mother. She had told him, "You're having a son that's being born in a few days; you need to be out here." So he came out. Fifty years later my eldest sister, Carolyn, told me that he told her, "I'm taking you to the hospital to see your baby brother." She's excited about it, but he tells her, "Don't tell your mom." Within the next few days, I get brought home. Mattie, my adoptive mother, lived in a two-story brick flat. My father, his fiancée, and my half-sisters were on the bottom floor, and Mattie and I were on the top floor.

We get home. She takes me upstairs and tells my sisters, "You guys be quiet. We don't want to wake the baby up." My dad does whatever he does. Carolyn goes downstairs and tells her sister Robbie, "There's a baby upstairs." Robbie says, "What?" Over the next couple days they get really excited and keep sneaking upstairs, and Mattie's saying, "Be quiet. Don't wake that baby up."

Carolyn and Robbie's mother finally says, "What is going on with y'all?"

"There's a baby upstairs."

"What do you mean there's a baby upstairs? Show me."

My sisters take her upstairs and show her. She walks in the room. As Carolyn told me, she took one look and said, "We're packing." They went downstairs, proceeded to pack, and left within a day or so, and didn't speak to my dad for a couple years. My dad left a few weeks after that, coming back to California. Since they were his daughters he had visitation rights, but that was the extent of it.

A few months later the flu pandemic of 1957 sweeps through Detroit, and Mattie quits her job in a Ford plant to go with my father back to Blevins, Arkansas, where her family is. My father owed Mattie for adopting me. She had bought the two-story brick flat after hitting the numbers, but she gave it to a family member and went to Blevins, because my grandfather was very ill, and because the flu pandemic was hitting its stride in Detroit. One day in downtown Blevins, my grandfather and my Uncle Albert are walking along, and a white man tells my grandfather to get off the sidewalk. My grandfather hesitates and resists, and the white man kicks the dog and utters a racial slur. My Uncle Albert steps in. A few days after that they catch my Uncle Albert in the woods, and these three white men are going to beat him. He ends up clubbing them. The story goes that he killed one or two of them.

The third one got away, but when Uncle Albert came back, he said, "I have to go." Because if he didn't leave, the Klan was going to harass or kill the whole family, which would mean my Aunt Emma, my Great-Aunt Rosie, my mother, and myself. So Uncle Albert left and went to Shreveport, Louisiana. My grandfather passes away soon after that, and my father shows up again and drives Mattie and me out to California. My mother Mattie never learned to drive a car, although she did know how to ride a horse sidesaddle. Probably another two years later there's a letter from my Uncle Albert saying, "They caught me. I'm in Shreveport, Louisiana. I don't know if I'll make it." That's the last contact any of us had with my Uncle Albert. By this time my mother and I are in Fresno, on the west side, living in I wouldn't call it a squatter camp, but there were little shacks all around.

In Fresno when I was growing up, in the sixties, you could choose to be part of the rest of the world or not. Those were turbulent years in the rest of the world. The Vietnam War was raging. Riots were happening in Watts and Detroit and Newark. LA and San Francisco were so polluted that people didn't want to live there. Black people were still being lynched in the South and murdered in the Northern cities. But Fresno was a protected environment for me. You had a choice whether you wanted to engage with the outside world, because you were in a farm town. If you were in the city, within minutes you could be in the country, driving past fields of cotton or corn or orchards of walnut or pecan or olive or apple or peach trees.

At any given time, there were thousands of immigrants in and around Fresno, picking a multitude of vegetables and fruits. By the time my mother and I arrived there, the earlier waves of Greeks and Italians, as well as Blacks, had moved up the social ladder, to be replaced in the menial agricultural jobs by migrant Mexicans and Central Americans. The community had a transitory vibe, because the migrant workers were always coming and going. You might make a friend and then not see him or her for a couple years. When you did, you might ask: "Where you been?" And the answer might be the Oregon border, or San Diego, or Temecula, or the San Fernando Valley. Fresno and the Central Valley of California have been crucial to feeding much of America and even the world for many decades, and the migrant workers who came and went, my childhood friends and neighbors, were and still are the backbone of that economy.

My mom moved there because her two older sisters were already there. Aunt Ruby and Aunt Mary had moved to Fresno, as far as I know, directly from Blevins, Arkansas. For whatever reason, a whole lot of my mother's family ended up in Fresno: the Simmons family, the Pennywells, the Watkins family, the Hunters, the Maxwells. Aunt Ruby married a Watkins. I think what attracted many of them was that Fresno was a farming community, like the communities they had come from in the South, and they could find their comfort zone within it, rather than battling the dangers and uncertainties of truly urban cities like San Francisco and Los Angeles.

My earliest memories are of living in a one-room shack behind a larger main house where Mr. and Mrs. Epps lived. I had to go to their house to bathe. I had a slop jar that I would use at night, because we didn't have indoor plumbing. To a kid, whatever environment you grow up in is your norm until you see something different. And in many ways, it was a wonderful place to be a kid. As I got older I was out hunting frogs and birds and making slingshots, making bows, creating arrows with old, rusty nails, building stuff. I thought we could actually dig to the middle of the earth, so me and my friends started digging in my backyard. We got about four feet down by three feet across and said, "Oh, it's too hard. We'll dig another day." And it was about running crazy in the country, eating loquats, picking fruit, picking vegetables, going to family reunions. There were things that just allowed me to be a kid. We lived on the west side, in this little one-room house. It's my normal, so it's okay. I'm playing with the kids next door, and there's one girl who's crippled with cerebral palsy. She was my first crush. I wanted to help her, and we played together for years.

When I was five, my mother was a member of Thomas Butler's church, Deliverance Temple. It was right on the west side, out in the country, and he did faith healings. And I had very bad bronchitis as a kid, as well as random bloody noses. I could only play for thirty-five or forty minutes at a time and then my mom would bring me inside, because either I would start gasping or my nose would start bleeding. One particular night we were in the church, and they would always have this blessed olive oil. And Thomas Butler calls me up, or my mother takes me up, and I don't know if she's asking for me to be healed or just saying that I'm sickly. But in any case, Thomas Butler puts the blessed oil on my forehead and makes a cross, and then he grabs my forehead and shakes me and does this type of prayer really quick and says, "He's healed."

After that a few more people are healed, a few people catch the Holy Ghost and they're rolling on the floor and whatnot, and the service ends. And after church there'd always be these fried chicken dinners, which I just loved, and we'd take some chicken home. But after that particular service, I never had a bronchitis attack again in my life. And I never had asthma in my life, and I was able to be a normal kid without having these bronchitis attacks. My nose still bled when I got overheated, but I no longer had bronchitis. So to say that I had seen faith healers before Jim Jones is an understatement. I'd been seeing faith healers since I was five years old. I was a sickly kid when I was really young, but after that I was fine. So I know that positive thought works as well, so that's all I've got to say about that.

Then I get ready for kindergarten, and I'm already reading. My mother read to me every day and made me read back to her and repeat the words, so when I got into kindergarten I knew how to read. My mom walks me to the kindergarten, drops me off at school, and goes to work. She's a domestic worker at that time. At kindergarten, I take all the toys from all the other kids. I get into the sandbox, and every time they tried to get into the sandbox with me, I'd push them out. The teacher comes out and says, "You have to share, Eugene."

I said, "No, I don't."

"Yes, you do."

"No, I don't."

It's a back and forth. Then after school she writes a note and says, "Take this home to your mother." This was 1962, and kids walked home in those days, even at five years old. So I'm walking home on a dirt road, like a little path to the school from where we lived, and I open up the letter, and I read it. It says, "Eugene doesn't play very well with others. He doesn't share." Well, I didn't like that, so I crumpled it up and threw it to the side and came on home. I went next door to Mr. Epps's house and stayed there until my mom got back. She said, "How was school?"

"School was great, fine day."

"You had fun?"

"Yeah, I had fun. It's good. Lots of kids."

The next day, she walks me to school and drops me off again and goes to work. The teacher says, "Where is your mother, Eugene?"

"She's where she's supposed to be."

"And where is that?"

"She's at work."

"Did you give her the letter I gave you yesterday?"

I said, "No, I didn't. I read it and I didn't like it."

At lunch, the teacher walks me home and drops me off at Mr. Epps's house. I don't know what was said, but I never went back to school again for another year and a half, until first grade. And within that year and a half, my mother got married. We moved into a traditional three-bedroom house with a fireplace. We had peach trees and loquat trees in the front. There were also plum trees and apricot trees. In a vacant lot next door to us was a pomegranate tree. Next to that lot was the Rodriguez family, who were Mexican. There was Anselmo Rodriguez and Johnny Rodriguez and Delia Rodriguez, and we were friends. We had fun competitions picking fruit.

My stepfather, Charles Gibson, was a Seventh-day Adventist, so we were Seventh-day Adventists, and I went to the Fresno Adventist Academy from first to sixth grade. I never knew how my mother met Mr. Gibson. Just one day, "I'm getting married. I want you to meet somebody," and that was it. I never called him Dad. I always called him Mr. Gibson, because he seemed so old in comparison to my mother. Nobody knows their mother's old unless she tells you, "I'm old." Other than that, she's always young. I thought my mom was young and that Mr. Gibson was really old. But they weren't that far apart in age. I don't know much about Mr. Gibson, except that during the years my mother was married to him, we were solidly middle class. My eldest stepbrother, Charles Gibson Jr., had gone to the Adventist Academy, and he'd also gone to Loma Linda University. He was a graduate. I had another older stepbrother, Rudolph Gibson, who was also adopted. He went as far as high school in the Adventist Academy, as far as I know. I don't think he went to college.

Back in Detroit, my mother had gone to all kinds of churches. She went to the Church of Our Prayers founded by Rev. James L. Lofton, who was a playboy minister in the fifties, and she went to Rev. C. L. Franklin's church, and she went to some Catholic church. And when she first adopted me, she took me to Rev. Lofton and he said, "He's gonna be a messenger." And she gave me every opportunity to be a messenger. Her message to me was: "You're gonna learn to read, you're gonna learn to write, you're gonna learn to communicate. You're not gonna be out there using slang. If you do, it'll be because you purposefully used it, not because you learned it." So she made sure that I went to the best schools that she could afford. At that time, that was the Adventist Academy, through her marriage to Charles Gibson.

I'm just old enough to remember the Kennedy assassination. I remember my mom coming to my auntie's house that was keeping me, my Aunt Mary. And my Aunt Mary's upset and my mom comes in and says, "They killed him. They killed the only good man alive." And she's crying. We walked home after that. I was in first grade at the time. It seems like the Kennedy assassination really affected my mom. And I suspect that was the first time she voted Democrat, because before that most Black folks voted Republican. It was Kennedy that changed that. But at that time, I didn't know what Republicans and Democrats were.

I knew that the Republican Party was Lincoln's party, so they must be okay. There weren't Democrats then, but Dixiecrats. My mom hated Dixie, but I didn't know what that was. I didn't really have a concept of it. "This is a Republican, this is a Dixiecrat." But Kennedy was a Democrat, and that was new. And he wasn't Southern. And my mom said, "That's a pretty man."

Because I'd been reading since I was five years old, reading at seven was a breeze. I had good relationships at the Academy. I went to church every Saturday morning, as Adventists do. I didn't look at TV from Friday night to Sunday night. She made sure I memorized the names of all the books of the Bible, because there was a test that you had to pass. Then in the evenings and on Sundays, I was a regular kid. I'd go outside and play and have fun with all the neighbor kids. A lot of them were Mexican-American, migrant workers who had finally saved up enough to get a house. The few Black friends I had were also Seventh-day Adventists. The Academy went from first to twelfth grade on the same campus, across the street from the zoo in Roeding Park. Only nine of us were Black in the whole school.

Behind our house, adjacent to a vacant lot, lived the Sykes family. I came to their attention when their second-oldest daughter, Lynda, started noticing me on a regular basis, sneaking through the fence into my back yard. There were six kids in the Sykes family, and Lynda was like the junior mother, the most self-sufficient member of the whole family. I think she thought I was homeless, because she never saw me with anyone. The real reason for that was that I wasn't allowed to play with kids in the neighborhood, the whole time I was going to the Academy. But Lynda was concerned for my well-being, and at some point she got her mom to agree to invite me in for dinner. The Sykes family ended up taking me in. They fed me. They allowed me to eat meat, which I hadn't eaten in five years because Adventists are vegetarians. Mr. and Mrs. Sykes always said, "You know you're welcome. Don't worry. You want to have dinner with us, sure." They were a large family, and I was an outlier, but they made me very welcome in their home. They weren't really relatives at all, but we were like an extended family. When I was maybe twelve they took me in and said, "Okay, you're part of the family." Mike was always working on cars, Lynda was always in the kitchen, Ann was always on the phone. Mike and Ann were close to my age, and we hung out. They were good country folk, and I became like a member of their family. This relationship carried on well into adult life. Even now, Lynda and I remain good friends. After I returned from Guyana she was protective of me, and it might not even be an exaggeration to say that she saved my life.

I wasn't really cognizant of color or race or anything, even though there was a white Seventh-day Adventist church and there was a Black Seventh-day Adventist church, and the two only met once a year. Other than that, the two congregations never mixed. But at school it was about education. They weren't pushing religion. They were pushing that you had to be educated. You had to read, you had to communicate, you had to be ready for the real world. The only way you could be ready was to be educated, and education didn't have a religion. We pledged allegiance to the flag every morning. I don't remember us doing prayers in school. What made the school so interesting was that, after we got out of school, we could run to the high school and look at all the science classes and experiments and bodies in formaldehyde and all that kind of stuff.

At the end of fifth grade, going into sixth, the school moved from Roeding Park out to Clovis. Up until this time I had all female teachers, and they all were good to me. They were decent to me. My first male teacher was Mr. Royer.

Mr. Royer took a difference to how we played flag football. We'd always tackle each other, but not maliciously or anything, and he would always tell me, "You're playing too rough, Eugene." I would explain to him: "We've been playing together for six years. We know each other. We wouldn't hurt each other. We're all friends. We just do this because it's fun." So he says, "You mind if I play?" "Okay, come on in and play." He was playing with us, and I ended up tackling him. He fell on the ground, and then he started going into a seizure. He started shaking. He was turning red and trembling and stuff. I'm on the ground on my knees trying to help him, and I can't. Then I'm starting to cry because, I mean, I've hurt this man. Then he jumps up and says, "See! Told you, that's why you don't play rough." And he started laughing at me. I went home that day, and I couldn't go back to school.

My mom said, "You don't feel well?"

"No, I don't feel well."

So she dropped me off at my Aunt Ruby's house. A few days passed, I'm still not feeling well, and my mom called Dr. Curry, the Black folks' doctor. He checked me out and said nothing was wrong. Another week passed, and my auntie started getting worried, like, "What's going on? He loves school. He loves studying. He loves reading. He loves it all." She asked me, "What's going on, Butch?"

I said, "I can't go back there. This is what he did to me."

She said, "That wasn't nice."

I said, "Don't tell my mother, because I don't want to fail her. I have to graduate. I can't fail her, but I just can't go back there." She tells my mother anyway, and all I know is I never went back to the Adventist Academy, but I got transferred to John Muir Elementary.

This is sixth grade. It was like the last semester and a half of school, so they say, "The only way he's gonna pass is, he has to make up a whole year's work. We're not accepting the transcripts." Or something. Those last twelve or fifteen weeks of school, that's all I did, was just come home and do homework. I was the first Black kid to go there. The other kids were Italian and Spanish, Mexican, Latino, multiple backgrounds, but I knew I was the only Black kid in the whole school. I'm in class, and the teacher's name was Mr. Harmon. He says, "This is Eugene. He's our new student. Please make him welcome." They start snickering. There's this kid in the back of the class named Gary Felix. I'll never forget him, because we became close friends all through junior high. He's doing something, and Mr. Harmon says, "Look, I need you to be quiet, Gary." Gary keeps doing whatever he's doing, and Mr. Harmon says, "I told you to shut up," which I'd never heard in a school. Teachers never said that at the Adventist Academy. Mr. Harmon stomps back there and snatches Gary up, literally shakes the desk off of him. He snatches him up so fast and says, "Go to the principal's office." I'm in shock, because this is unheard of. This doesn't happen in private school.

Later I'm walking down the hall, and this big kid behind me, Manuel Frutos, is thumping me on the back of my head. This kid is huge, like 160 pounds in the sixth grade. I turn around, and he thumps the middle of my forehead. I steel myself. I'm looking at him, and with all my might I take a swing at him. He looks at me and says, "I'll see you in the pool after school, fool." What the hell is the pool after school? Well, I found out it was a wading pool that was only open during the summertime, for summer school for the small kids. What you did was, you got in the middle of the pool, and they surrounded the pool so you couldn't get out. That's where the fight went forth. Now I'm rattled, on my first day of school. I just want to get home. I have to catch a bus I'm not familiar with; there's no car picking me up like at the Academy. No car dropping me off, no support system. I don't know anybody. My logic is that, if I try to run to the bus stop and they catch me, they'll kill me. Which they wouldn't—they'd just beat the hell out of me. But you're in sixth grade.

Out of fear, after school I go to the pool, and I wait. And I wait. Kids come around, but Manuel Frutos doesn't show up, because nobody had ever challenged him before. I'm standing in the pool out of stupidity and fear, not out of bravery. I don't want to get chased down the street. I don't want to get beat up at the bus stop. At least if I get beat up at school, maybe a teacher will step in and save me. But Manuel never showed. I walk to the bus stop looking over my shoulder. I get on the bus looking over my shoulder. The bus takes off, and I'm safe. I said to myself, "I survived." Then I said, "Oh man, tomorrow's gonna be worse."

I didn't tell my mom. "How was school?"

"School was fine."

I come to school the next day, and I'm a hero. I'm a fucking hero. Everybody's talking to me like, "Hey, Eugene, right on, man." It's like, what? Now I had friends to walk to the bus stop with me. Manuel never says nothing to me again.

School was okay for the next few weeks, and then there was a kid I got into it with. His name was Mickey Anderson. Started throwing rocks. I'd been throwing rocks forever, so I threw a rock and hit him. The other kids said, "His dad said to kick your ass." I wasn't as scared of Mickey as I was of Manuel, because now I had friends. So I beat him up, and I walked to the bus stop again. It was okay after that.

I graduated and made it to seventh grade. It was 1969, the first year of school busing in Fresno. Now I'm coming into contact with other Black kids, who wonder who I am. They're saying, "Where do you live?"

"I live on East Geary."

"We never seen you before."

"That's because I went to another school."

"You talk strange."

"I don't know."

"Okay. So who do you know?"

"I know that guy. I know Raymond."

"Squirrel, come over here."

"That's Butch. Yeah, he went to private school."

"Oh, okay."

And they left me alone for the most part. They called Raymond Squirrel because he used to hunt squirrels, and thought he shot one, but he didn't. It bit the shit out of him, so they called him Squirrel. So I reacquaint myself with Squirrel, Floyd, Mitchell, Bishop, Ronald. We get BB guns after school, and we start hunting birds.

So I had some cred because somebody knew me from the neighborhood, even though I wasn't allowed to play with kids in the neighborhood, because I went to private school and my mom despised the parents of the other Black kids because she felt they could have done more for their kids and didn't. So now I get reacquainted with kids I had known in the neighborhood, and junior high is okay. I get teased a little bit, but not much. I stick to my studies. And I wasn't aware of my color, that I was different, until one day I'm on the field and Terry Trovato calls me a nigger. I didn't know what that was, so I went home and asked my mom: "What's a nigger?"

"That's somebody dumb, stupid, and ignorant," she tells me. "Why?"

"Oh, nothing. Just wanted to know."

Never heard the word before. I heard either Black or Negro, and I didn't particularly care for Negro. Black made sense to me, but I didn't associate with it, because I'm Eugene. I come back to school the next day, and during PE I proceed to kick Terry Trovato's ass, I mean literally kick his ass. I didn't punch him. I just kicked him. I kicked him across the track field, up the ramp, past the wood shop and the gymnasium. He's running away from me, and I'm running up and kicking him. "This is for dumb, stupid, and ignorant. I'll show you who's dumb, stupid, and ignorant." We're both in seventh grade. Nothing happened. The Black kids thought I was great. That was my street cred for the Black kids. In the process of that I finally became the individual, Eugene. These Black kids teased me because of the way I communicated, the white kids teased me because of the color I was. So I was in no man's land, with the exception of the Latinos, who didn't really care how I talked or what color I was. Just, "Hey, you play football, you play basketball, let's go." I made friends with them and stayed friends with them and a few Italians: Diana Benedetti, Thomas Panzarino. They seemed to be on the outside looking in, the same as I was. And they both seemed to be individuals, rather than followers. Hamilton Junior High, where I went to school, is in an Italian section. There's whole districts of Italians and Greeks in Fresno, which are still there, although maybe not in the same numbers.

That's when I became color conscious, aware that I was obviously different. And, even though I had Black friends, they weren't that friendly towards me, because of my language skills. The white boys were ambivalent towards me, because, "Who does he think he is, talking like that?" And the white girls were like, "He's cute, but he's different." So the only friends I had were the Latino kids until, in eighth grade, I finally made a real good friend, Thomas Panzarino, and we were really cool through junior high and high school.

When I got into ninth grade, I felt that Martin Luther King's birthday should be a holiday, so I organized a march. I said, "We're leaving at lunch. If you don't leave at lunch, I'm gonna come into class and drag you out." This was January 1972. I told them that if they didn't walk out of class, we were going to kick their asses the next day. When lunchtime came, it's like, "Come on, let's go." We all walked off the school grounds and down to the bus stop and caught the bus downtown to Fresno Mall. We didn't know what to do. We just knew that we had to leave school. We went to Perry Boys Smorgy. I think it was like a dollar ninety-nine for all you can eat. So we go to Perry Boys Smorgy and we eat up. We go home at the regular time. Didn't tell our parents. Next day we go to school, and the truant officer is there, Mr. Finley. He says, "I'll let you guys get away with this. I could've arrested all of you." And we snickered. Mr. Finley was Black, and everybody hated him because whenever you skipped school he was the guy that would pick you up and take you to your parents and make sure they beat you. He said, "I didn't want to do it, but don't do it again." Then we're all let out of the library to go back to class. That was my introduction to politics, and understanding that when you take a stand, other people take a stand too, and their stand most likely is going to be against what you're standing for.

I watched the news growing up, but in terms of political conversations that my mom and Mr. Gibson would have, it wasn't that I wasn't allowed to be part of them, I just wasn't. It wasn't discussed at dinner. It was discussed after dinner, when I'd be doing my homework or playing with the dog or the cat or whatever, and they would get into political discussions. So I wasn't politicized. I didn't become politicized until I was fourteen years old. At fourteen I'm starting to see all these different riots throughout the country, and the Vietnam War. And then I organized that walkout, because I thought Martin Luther King's birthday should be a holiday.

In the picture for my ninth-grade graduation from Hamilton Junior High that year, 1972, I'm in the fifth row up, with my arms crossed and the two fingers like Wakanda on my shoulders, and my middle fingers. The first two hundred copies that came out showed my fingers. When I looked at it later in high school, they had fizzed it out or something. I laughed at that.

CHAPTER 4
Allowed to Speak Out

Sometime during the summer of 1972, between ninth and tenth grade, the year I turned fifteen and started at Fresno High, my mother tells me she's heard of a man called Jim Jones, and that I might find him interesting. So I go to a meeting, at Irwin Junior High School in Fresno.

It's sort of interesting, but more interesting were all the young people and how focused they were. It's like they knew what they were doing and where they were going. They communicated. They didn't seem afraid of anything. The girls were different from the girls I had seen. The boys and young men were completely different. They didn't seem to be impressed by anything, but they seemed to have some type of focus. That was interesting.

Jones himself was at that meeting, and he was doing healings. But I wasn't paying attention to that, because my mom had been to so many churches, and I'd seen plenty of healers before. I'd seen guys that forecast the future and all of that, so that wasn't impressive to me. In seventh grade, Bishop Brown had brought an *Ebony* magazine to school, and it showed a Black Jesus. That had made me say to myself: They fucking lied to me. It wasn't that I became an atheist, but I definitely became an agnostic. I'm questioning this shit. The Adventists had lied to me, and the Baptists had lied to me. The Jehovah's Witnesses had lied to me. The storefront preachers had lied to me. Rev. Lofton and Rev. Franklin in Detroit. They all had lied to my mother. They told her that Jesus was blond-haired and blue-eyed. He's not, and here's proof. I was mad. I was really pissed off because I had been tricked, and I felt they had tricked my mom as well. Now Jim Jones comes up, and he's healing and stuff. It's like, well, is this real or not? I didn't know.

My mom decides that we should give Jones's church a try. "Want to go up there for the summer, to Redwood Valley?" I say, "I don't mind." My cousin Clarence is a member, so he drives us up to Redwood Valley, where Peoples Temple was based at the time, and we stay in Ukiah with Temple member Penny Kerns.

I took my steamer with me, a real big trunk like people used to take on ships. Mike and Albert Touchette, their dad, their mother, Jack Beam, Rheaviana Beam, they're all up there, and I start helping them work on a catfish pond that's right outside the convalescent home owned by the Temple. We go up to the Redwood Valley church, swim in the pool, but the main thing was building a catfish pond around the convalescent home. This was supposed to create another food supply, along with grapes that were being grown by the Temple and different food crops. Beau is up there too, and we're working on this pond every day, sweating. I'm losing all my baby fat, and I'm getting excited, because this is really cool. I'm fucking nasty. I'm doing a good thing, and it's like, "Yeah, this is kind of fun, I like this." They're operating the equipment, and I want to learn how to do that too. So it was exciting. It's like, "Right on! These are white people doing it." All I had ever seen were Black farmers. I'd never seen white farmers before. I didn't even know white people farmed. I thought they went to the grocery store. We farmed. White people went to the grocery store, because they had money. But here, white people were doing something I was accustomed to.

One afternoon I come home, to Penny Kerns's house on North State Street in Ukiah. My mom makes me some kind of little snack, and her and Penny are talking, and Penny wants her to do something, and Mom says no. A slight argument or something. And Penny says something to the effect of, "You're so damn lazy." My mom had worked all my life. She'd cleaned up other people's houses. I'd met those people, and they were nice, but she was still a domestic. I didn't look down on that. I looked up to it, because she did all that for me. So now with Penny, I lost it. I got up from the table, walked up, pushed her head against the wall, and I'm strangling her. I'm telling her, "Don't you ever call my mother lazy. She's anything but lazy." My mom's begging me, "Please don't kill this white woman, Eugene. Do not kill this white woman. Do not kill this white woman. Please baby, don't kill her, Eugene, don't hurt her. She didn't know what she said. She didn't mean it."

"Yes she did," I say.

"No I didn't, no I didn't," says Penny.

So I let her go, and she slumps. And she runs out of the house with her Doberman pinscher that she adopted from the SPCA. Those were the days when you had Doberman pinschers turning on their owners from being inbred and stuff. And she drives to the Temple and immediately reports me to Jim Jones. I take my shower and get washed up. Somebody comes by, and they pick us up for the meeting that night. And in the meeting Jones says, "Oh, I saved your life today, Penny. That Doberman pinscher you got was gonna attack you, and I prevented that from happening, and blah blah blah." The Doberman pinscher was me. As the meeting finished that night, one of Jones's confidants told me, "We'd like for you to leave, you and your mother." So I gave them the middle finger, and we packed up all our stuff that night and left the next morning, back to Fresno. And I said, "I'm not gonna take that." So I didn't really go back to the Temple until twelfth grade.

In eleventh grade, the dean got tired of me acting out and telling the teachers what they should be teaching. He said, "Eugene, I'm not kicking you out of Fresno High. I'm kicking you out of the school district." That was serious, and he knew it was serious. It was like getting sent to prison, because he knew I would have no voice. In those days, people still paid for things with money orders. So my mom would give me money orders to pay her bills. I always kept the carbons. So I forged her signature and transferred myself to predominantly Black Edison High on the west side. Now I was going to school four blocks from home, whereas all my life I'd been going to school across town, but I was leaving home in the morning at the same time. And she didn't know it for like three months. When she found out she said, "Just graduate. If you just graduate, that's all I'm asking." And that was intended as an impetus, like, "I need to find a focus for him." I think in her mind, Peoples Temple worked for that too. Her fear was that I would become like the other Black kids in the neighborhood.

My mother continued to go to Peoples Temple meetings. I said, "Fuck it. I'm not going back. And if I do go back, it's gonna be on my terms." I'd go to a few meetings, between tenth and twelfth grade, in San Francisco or LA. It was cool because I'd want to go shopping, so I would get me some clothes from San Francisco, some shoes from LA, because you couldn't get those in Fresno. I was getting my clothes from out of town.

The Temple had twelve Greyhound buses. They would stop in Fresno to pick up Temple members every Saturday morning early, like 4:00 a.m., and go either up to San Francisco or down to Los Angeles. Occasionally, there'd be one going to Redwood Valley. There were well over sixty or seventy members getting on the bus in Fresno. When we were going to LA, we would stop in Buttonwillow. That would be the break. Everybody get out, stretch their legs, play football or whatever.

By the time I was in twelfth grade, I pretty much hadn't gone to any churches in a couple years. My mom had gone to multiple churches, but I didn't, because I was tired of it. When I was in twelfth grade she told me, "Well, I'm moving up to San Francisco. Do you want to go?" I'm eighteen, and it's the summer of '75 going into the winter of '76, and I was already attending Fresno City College. I said okay. "Yeah, I'll move up there. That sounds okay." I graduated high school in '75, and we moved up probably in January of '76.

A lot of things happened in those next two years, between '76 and '78. I was in charge of the construction crew, I got married. I mean, those two years were just filled.

My mother gave our house in Fresno to Peoples Temple, and Walter "Smitty" Jones, who left the Temple the following summer and married the high-profile defector Grace Stoen, came down from Redwood Valley and brought the construction crew to start rehabbing it to be sold. One weekend I was still there at the house, and the crew left their van. It was one of those Scooby-Doo vans. "Oh, I'm taking this for a spin." I take it for a spin and burn the clutch out. Well, didn't burn it out totally, but it was smelling pretty bad. I parked it back, and the next weekend was when we actually moved up to the city and the Temple took possession of the house. No one ever said anything about me and the van, but my first day in the Temple they called me up to the third floor. I didn't know what the third floor was. It was where Jones and his immediate family stayed, on the third floor at the San Francisco Temple, on Geary Avenue between Steiner and Fillmore.

The Temple building in San Francisco was a former synagogue and Scottish Rite Masonic temple, and it was large enough to have a sanctuary plus several floors of apartments and meeting rooms. I go up to the third floor, and Maria Katsaris and Anita Ijames are there. "Okay, Eugene. You're here now. You're a socialist, and we're not gonna have you carousing all these girls and women and whatnot. Those days are over with. You're gonna be a worker now." I'm listening to them, and I'm thinking, "I only wish I could carouse these girls." They said, "You're gonna be on the work crew. We'll take you downstairs, introduce you to Jack Beam." I meet with Jack Beam and I'm thinking, "Aw man, this old white guy, this isn't gonna go well."

He says, "Hey Eugene. How you doing?"

"I'm doing all right," I say.

He puts his arm around me and says, "Don't sweat it. It's gonna be okay." He starts walking me around and introducing me to different guys. "This is Poncho. This is Calvin. That's Jimmy Jr., that's Stephan." I knew who the Jones boys were, but there was never a formal introduction. I sensed them to be spoiled brats. I wasn't aware of Jones's complete extended family: Tim "Day" Jones (who was white and called Tim Day to distinguish him from Tim "Night" Jones, who was Black); Suzanne and Lew, who were Korean. I became aware of them over the following days and weeks.

So I started working on the construction crew, and it was fun. I enjoyed it. I guess Guyana was becoming more than a dream for them at that time, although I wasn't aware of it. The Peoples Temple Agricultural Project—what came to be called Jonestown—was established around this time by a group of Temple members known as the pioneers, who cleared 3,800 acres in the jungle in northwest Guyana, near the Venezuelan border. On the construction crew in San Francisco we were making crates to be shipped out of the country, but I didn't know or care where they were going. This is the winter of '76. I've dropped out of Fresno City College and I'm living in the Temple, on the second floor behind the stage. It was just like it was later in Jonestown: The more you're trusted, the further away you can get from the power. The less trusted you are, the closer you should be, because they want to indoctrinate you. So there were little apartments backstage, directly beneath the third floor where the Jones family lived, and above the dining room. And that's where I was living. Ted Holiday was living back there too, and another guy named Arthur. It was kind of cool.

I didn't know what PC was yet, and I found out because I could hear them thumping and wrestling or whatever, when somebody was getting disciplined in the middle of the night. PC was the Planning Commission. It was that, but it was also a disciplinary group. Their disciplinary actions went much further than the public disciplinary actions. These are people fighting. On Wednesday nights there were members-only meetings, where there was what was called catharsis. That meant that, if you had done something wrong in their eyes, you were called on the floor, as it was termed, and confronted with it. And you did not defend yourself. You just took it. You accepted it. You made your amends, and either you got a punishment, be it physical or working for the next twenty-four hours, or you did something magnanimous. "You're gonna work with the seniors." Fine, whatever.

By that time Jones's sermons had also changed, because he had become housing commissioner for the City of San Francisco, which is why we had all the communes. By that time, everything was changing. It started out with the fiery sermons and the healings, then later it became politicized: understanding that your vote counts, that we must demonstrate, we must represent, we must take up the cause for people who can't take up the cause for themselves. That appealed to me. Now, you can be a hero. Before, you were just an individual. But if you're helping somebody, and you're helping out of the goodness of your heart, that makes you a hero. Nobody has to know it, but you know it. "I'm doing this for the right reasons."

I felt that this was what this country needed. This capitalistic society would not continue like this. They were beating us and killing us—just like right now, half a century later. The police were pulling us over and jacking us over for no reason. It was crazy in LA at that time, let alone what was happening in the Fillmore in San Francisco, because the police were out there on a regular basis. They were running raids nightly in San Francisco and Los Angeles, where the two main Temples were. At that point Jones hadn't abandoned Redwood Valley, but Redwood Valley was like the safe haven. The fight was in the city, and that was where we needed to be, in the action.

I had come a long way from Fresno. I didn't like Fresno, because all I did there was get bloody noses. Not because I was getting beat up, but because it was so freaking hot that I got overheated and would get a bloody nose, which they told me later was a vitamin B deficiency of some type. I was just tired of it, and tired of the heat. Also the nation was changing, but Fresno was stuck in time.

But Fresno was behind me now. We call it NoTown or Fresnowhere.

I was seeing more of the world, at least the small world of California. I was becoming informed on a different level. I was being pushed by the Temple to learn more. I was listening to newscasts. I was listening to talk radio. I was looking at television, but now I'm looking at television to observe, not to be entertained. I'm walking the streets of San Francisco. I'm being politicized. I'm seeing politicians like Jerry Brown and Mervyn Dymally at Temple meetings. I'm seeing celebrities like Jane Fonda and Esther Rolle at meetings.

As weird as it was, it started becoming normal. And it's like, "Well, these people are more intelligent than I am, or at least they should be, or at least they seem to be." Even though there were cruel things happening during the members' meetings on Wednesdays, there were all these other things that were positive. It wasn't so much that the good things offset the cruel things, but they camouflaged them. People stood up in meetings and said, "I didn't have this, and now I do." And, "Yes, I donated my property, but I'm living in comfort. I'm not living in danger. I'm not living in fear." And I had classes that I could attend. Don Jackson taught me photography. Tim Clancy taught me how to operate a printing press. John O'Connell taught me shoe repair. Harry Williams taught me plumbing. Mr. Garrison taught me roofing. Ken Norton taught me in the wood shop.

I have friends. I have people of the same ilk communicating with me, and I can walk down the street and not be scared. It wasn't like that in Fresno, because in Fresno people were demonstrating, and the police were taking an offensive role. In Fresno, officers were getting rowdy. All of a sudden, "Oh, you don't want to be on this side of town after seven o'clock." Or "If you're on that side of town, make sure you catch the bus or a car. You don't want to be walking."

Fresno's a more conservative place, and the police have free rein there. They're dealing with a lot of Southern African Americans, and they're dealing with an immigrant group that doesn't have citizenship. Neither group can speak out. That's different from San Francisco, where you have an attitude that you're in a metropolitan area and you're allowed to speak out. There are other people who will speak out with you, whom you don't know. Fresno at that time was very cliquish, and there were no pro-Black groups that I knew of. When I was in ninth grade, they put us all in the library and Mr. Finley, the truant officer, came out and told us that he could've arrested all of us for walking out of school in support of making

Martin Luther King's birthday a holiday. Bullshit, but the comfort zone was there for him to say that.

But Fresno was changing, or else I was becoming more aware. I wasn't an innocent kid in private school anymore, plus it was now the midseventies. And school busing was still somewhat new and being tested daily. White parents in Fresno were mad about busing, because now their daughters or sons had Black boyfriends or girlfriends. There was a Chinese girl that I really liked. Her father was a sheriff, and she told him. He says, "You can't talk to him no more. He's Black." In seventh, eighth, and ninth grade these things were already happening, but I wasn't aware of it, because I was still acclimating from coming out of a parochial school. Terry Trovato kind of opened my eyes when he called me a nigger. I should actually thank him. I should still kick his ass again, but I should thank him and then kick his ass. In Oakland at that time, the Black Panthers were happening. We were aware of the Panthers. They weren't in Fresno as far as I knew. I'm sure there was a contingent there, but I was too young and not connected enough in that particular group to know about it. Peoples Temple allowed me to be that revolutionary that I couldn't be before in Fresno, because I had nobody else to be that with me.

By that time, Jones had dropped most of the religious theology and had become all about politics and socialism. That was excellent with me, because I knew that capitalism didn't work, or at least I assumed capitalism didn't work, because I looked around me and saw the results of it. Now, I feel that capitalism doesn't work completely, but I'm still here and that counts for something. But I was raised up with guys that I'd only see every couple years because they were picking fruits and vegetables up and down the whole coast. What that means to me about capitalism is that they have to follow a foodstuff to make a living, versus being able to make a living where they want to live. Something is wrong with that. The fact that your child can't go to school continuously because you have to follow a crop means that your child's missing out on a whole lot of things, just the interaction for one, but also they're not getting educated. During their formative years, they're picking up only bits and pieces of education. From twelve through eighteen, they're picking fruits and vegetables when they should be learning, but they can't, because their family can't survive on one person picking fruits and vegetables. It has to be everybody in the family. They have big families so they can make more money.

When I was at the Adventist Academy, the migrant kids' situation meant nothing to me, because I didn't understand it, because I wasn't around them during the day. In my younger years I'd only see them when I came home from school and played with them an hour or so before doing my homework, eating dinner, and going to bed. Once I got into junior high I was cognizant, but it still didn't really affect me. When I got into high school is when it became crystal clear that they were not being treated the same. That was when the white kids would call them wetbacks and spics and whatever derogatory term that an Italian or a Greek or just a standard Caucasian came up with to describe a group of people. That's what I was hearing. Only some of the Italians and Greeks had legal status, by the way. Not all. You had wops without official papers. The father of one of my friends didn't have official papers, even though he'd been here for decades. But this was the '70s, so the immigration thing wasn't a big thing, and the San Joaquin Valley was the breadbasket of America. It was like, "We don't care where you're from, just pick this shit."

One thing I knew from early on was that without farmers, you can't have a nation. At the turn of the twentieth century, there were over a million Black farmers. There are fewer than ten thousand now. They weren't all sharecroppers. Many were actually farmers that owned their land, in the South, and some out here too. My relatives by adoption all had farmland. It didn't get passed on, because none of the younger generation wanted to farm it, and I wasn't close enough to them to qualify. Because I was in the Temple and overseas at the time they passed away, I had no access to the land. If I had, I would've taken it. I would've taken the skills I learned as a kid and developed them. But my cousins felt that was beneath them: "I don't want to be a farmer; I don't want to be out there sweating. I want to get an office job. Anything but farming." To this day they haven't succeeded, but they had the foundation of wealth, and they just let it go.

Anyway, Beau had become my best friend in the summer of '72, the same summer I choked Penny Kerns, the summer we worked on the catfish pond at the convalescent home in Redwood Valley. We were digging it every day, with Mike and Albert Touchette. The way Beau and I ended up being best friends was that I came into the Temple one afternoon, prior to choking Penny of course, and there was a fight going on. Beau was whooping Tim Jones's ass, over by the boys' bathroom in the Redwood Valley Temple by the pool. I'm observing this, and everybody grabbed

Beau, but they didn't grab Tim. I said, "Wow, that's kind of chickenshit. But you know what? Brother-man's got enough for himself." So I thought that was really good. Beau and I ended up being best friends for years after that, and we also challenged the hierarchy of the Jones boys.

It wasn't that the Jones boys were aggressive; they were just arrogant spoiled brats, and they felt the need to express and exhibit their hierarchy. I wasn't accepting that, and Beau wouldn't accept it either. Luckily enough we both had a savior, Jack Beam. Because Beau and I were good workers, because we understood construction, we understood creating working relationships that were friendships as well, we had dynamic construction crews. There was always the challenge of who's going to get noticed and who's not going to get noticed. We were aggressive. We had fights, not amongst each other but with other folks, and we didn't get disciplined for it. It put us on a pedestal, but at the same time it made us objects of "We have to find a way to get these guys"—which fortunately never really happened.

The Jones boys had their friends, and we had ours. We were competing. One of their friends was Jackie Colbert. The buses would always go up to San Francisco or down to LA, and sometimes people would get left in one or the other city. One time, had to be mid-1976, the bus went down to LA and I was left in San Francisco, so Beau had no coverage on the construction crew in LA. Jimmy, Johnny Cobb, and Jackie Colbert felt the need to confront Beau: "Your buddy's not here, blah blah blah." There was no fight or anything, but Beau tells me, when he gets back to San Francisco on Sunday, "Yeah, man, these guys tried to jack me up."

"Really? Don't worry, we'll handle that." So we're coming back from one of the food warehouses, and we see Jackie Colbert walking up Steiner Street. "Yeah. Let's get him." So we pull over and we didn't beat him up, but we gave him, should I say, assertive threats. Then we left. Then we went back to the Temple an hour later, and Ava Cobb meets us on the second floor. She has a bat in her hand, she has Johnny and all them with her, and she's screaming at us. Somebody stepped in and defused the situation, because I wasn't backing down, and Ava was a councilor at that time, a member of PC, the Planning Commission. She was very up in the hierarchy, because she came from Indiana. Here I was, a kid from Fresno, and Beau, a kid from San Francisco, and we're challenging the hierarchy, and we weren't backing down.

Jones didn't call us on the floor or anything. We went to the next Wednesday night meeting, and there was no speech about it. It seems like Jack Beam put his thumb on it and that was the end of it. But from then on, we definitely had an enemy in Ava. It was easy to make enemies in the Temple. It was just a matter of what position those people were at that you made enemies of. I challenged the hierarchy because I figured if the hierarchy wasn't working as hard as I was, then they weren't setting an example. If you're not setting an example, I have nothing to follow. Therefore, you're going to get respect based on being just a human being, but not for your position. Most of the time, when I had fights or situations or scenarios in the Temple, I was very aggressive. I made my presence known. In some ways, it made things difficult. But in the end, it was probably one of the things that saved me. It's probably also, in the end, one of the things that has allowed me to survive more than forty years after the fact. If I'm truly afraid of something, or I'm not sure of it, I face it immediately, just so I can put it behind me, rather than waiting for something to happen. Once it's at my back, I've dealt with it, I've created a strategy for it, I understand it.

That's how it was in the Temple. It wasn't what you would do, it was what they thought you would do. Because everything was based on, "How do we perceive this person? How do we manipulate him or her? How do we get the best out of them? How do we get dedication out of them? How do we get work out of them?" There was always a psychological game going on. Jones would preach from the pulpit, and there'd be these threats coming out, and on the surface the threats were against the system outside the Temple. But in reality, he was telling individuals within the Temple certain things: "Back off, back up, calm down, do this, do that."

In the early to midseventies, Peoples Temple had been more religious in content, with healings and forecasts and that type of thing. Then Jones became more political when he became housing commissioner in San Francisco and his wife Marceline was inspecting convalescent homes, which is why we had the bevy of seniors in the Temple. By '76 there was no religion; it was strictly revolution at that point. It was either fight or flight, and Jones chose flight by going to Guyana. There was also the fight over the custody of little John Victor Stoen, who might have been Jones's son. That initiated a lot. Also, Jones had been caught in a bathroom in a theater in LA, propositioning an undercover vice cop. And the press, which he had managed so well for years, began to realize that there were big stories behind the Temple's façade. There were also disputes within the Temple over tax difficulties and financial improprieties. So Jones was in trouble in California, and he was not willing to face it. People will tell you that when Jones wasn't there, Jonestown was fantastic. It was when he was there for any period of time that things changed. Things got really bad when they told him, "You can't leave Guyana. You can't go back." He said, "That's no problem." The Guyanese told him, "You don't understand. If you're spotted anywhere but Jonestown, you're toast, you're out of here." At that point he needed a deflection, a disruption of some type. That's how the atmosphere in Jonestown became more and more antagonistic and heavy on the shoulders, like a yoke.

A lot of times Jones didn't even make sense, he was so drugged up. That was the head of the serpent, and some people wouldn't recognize the serpent without the head. "Without Jim Jones, this can't go on." Other people said, "We'll do better without him, we can make this work, because right now he's just background noise anyway." The seniors didn't feel the same. I could look at my mom and just see that she couldn't return to the States. Pop Jackson, who was eighty-five years old, same thing. He couldn't return. Because all you heard was about how bad the US was. "I can't go back to that." The religion got taken over by the politics, but ultimately everything got taken over by Jones's megalomania. People came to the Temple at different periods, so you see what you want to see.

For me at this point, the midseventies, it was no longer about marching, it was no longer about demonstrating, canvassing, or sending letters. It was to the point now where it was like, "Okay, I can go out here and fight for what I believe in. Cuba will give me that experience." That was it. It was a real simple thought to me. It wasn't a long, thought-out, sophisticated process or anything. It was what I wanted to do. I didn't want to be in Jonestown, I didn't want to be in a fucking agricultural mission. I wanted to be on the front line. To me, Jonestown was a means to an end.

With Peoples Temple you were always running into spooks, whether they were CIA, FBI, some kind of governmental whatever, or some military guy. I couldn't prove it, but I knew it. Because the Temple was so outspoken in the Fillmore in San Francisco, you were identified. When we walked down the street, people knew who we were. A guy tried to snatch Ollie's purse on Fell Street. I chased him up the hill into his house and said, "Do you know who the fuck I am?" He knew. That was the brazenness that we had. Stephan Jones got into an issue with some kind of Chinese gang, and a few members and Johnny Brown had to go down and make peace with them. It wasn't like they didn't know who we were, because we were brazen; we weren't scared of anything, because we were Peoples Temple. We came from LA, we came from Detroit, we came from New Jersey, we came from San Francisco, we came from Compton, we came from Richmond—and we'll all come together on your ass. You don't disrespect us, you don't disrespect or touch or speak to our women. We made ourselves a threat in the Fillmore, and we challenged gang members, even in LA.

It was almost like we were a street gang, even when we went to Chicago on cross-country trips. We had a guy that was a former leader in what became the Blackstone Rangers. We had Temple members that had been in upper echelons of gangs, so we had their rep with us. It's like, "Oh, yeah. Come on man, let's go to the projects. No problem, you're with me. Got you covered." We went to Cabrini Green to pamphlet. That's why I said there was no fear. We outnumbered anybody out there. Young Black guys, and white guys too, because they weren't allowed to be white comfortably. Being white bought them privilege, so deny your fucking privilege and get on the bandwagon. That's how that went. We're socialists. And we protect our own. We are better than them. They're outsiders. We're inside, we're here. We have what they need. We don't need them, they need us.

That came from Jones too. He would say: "We're better. That's why you're here." If there was an issue at the high school, we showed up. Like I said, everybody had their fighting skills on. I think Jones tried to masquerade his rough childhood in Indiana. He'd bring it up in sermons and whatnot, but his childhood was not the focus, and he made sure it was not the focus. What was the focus was that he'd broken away from the Disciples of Christ and founded the interracial Peoples Temple, and he and his wife were the first white couple in Indiana to adopt a Black baby, Jim Jones Jr. That in itself says a lot, right, wrong, or indifferent. Where it gets murky is where he was selling monkeys and going to Brazil and back. It's like, how'd this fucking get into this? That type of thing was baffling.

That wasn't an interest of mine. I didn't really care where he came from; I just needed to know where we were going. I think that was the essence for a lot of us young folks in the Temple.

We wanted to have emergency food. We had food stashed at Potrero Hill. We had food stashed in the Fillmore. We had stuff stashed in the Mission District. Wherever there was a commune, or someone had a garage, that was a food warehouse. This was non-perishable food, so it was heavy. Canned foods and stuff like that. Sometimes they said it was a necessity. They didn't say it was for an emergency, they just said it was a necessity. Just in case. So we handled it as such, but we weren't allowed to really talk about it. Ruby Carroll, Anita Ijames, Rheaviana Beam, and Pat Hess purchased it. We packaged it, moved it, transported it, stored it, stacked it, covered it up, camouflaged it. I don't even know what happened to all that food after we left. I'm sure somebody had food for years. It was a lot of food, just in case. I'm still like that. You don't wait for it to happen, you prepare for it to happen. If it doesn't happen, that's good. If it does happen, still good because you're prepared for it. There's a life lesson there.

I think the outside public thinks that we all got along, we all loved each other, we were all on the same page. We weren't. We were just like society. Some agreed, some didn't agree. Some fought, some didn't fight. Some wanted peace, some wanted war. There are always people that are like, "My life isn't good enough, I need to be in your business." There were gossipers too. Everything in society was represented in Peoples Temple in a microcosm. I could mingle, come in contact with over a thousand people in a week, and never talk to a person from the outside. Then you're seeing these politicians or community leaders or movie stars, coming to the Temple at odd times. Even though you were surrounded by constant madness, it was tempered by outsiders coming in and not recognizing that it was madness and seeing it as something good. That validates and normalizes it. People who wouldn't buy into it bought into it then. People like Jerry Brown and George Moscone and Jane Fonda validated it or bought into it to an extent. They saw it as resistance, as a radical critique of mainstream society. And it was resistance. It morphed over time. When I initially got introduced to the Temple, in ninth grade, Jones was doing lots of healings and telling people's futures. "On this day, this might happen to you, so don't do this, don't do that." I'll give you a perfect example. One Sunday night in Fresno, my mom came home and told me she had passed the cancer. There's a pregnant pause. I looked at her. I didn't know if Jones was fake or not; it just didn't appeal to me. She said, "No, I passed the cancer, Eugene. And he told me to tell you don't be playing over by this house down the street, because something's gonna happen there."

I'd been around faith healers all my life. I'd been around people making prophecies and stuff. We'd been in a multitude of churches, and I'd heard it all before. On my side of the street where I grew up in Fresno, going toward where he prophesied something would happen, there was a vacant lot, and then there was Mr. Rodriguez's house, and then there was a church on the corner. Then you crossed the street, and there was another house that was elevated a little bit. Jones said that was where it was going to happen. I had walked up and down that street who knows how many times, from first grade to twelfth grade. Nobody sped around there. You couldn't. A few weeks later somebody lost control of their car, ran up on the curb, and ran into the front of the house where I always used to be hanging out. Now that was interesting. It's like, "Huh. Okay." I had to weigh that.

Soon after that I started junior college at Fresno City College. Then my mom said she was moving to San Francisco, did I want to go, and I said yes.

What I found out years later was that sometimes in the Temple, houses would be broken into. Your house might be broken into, and it was a way of finding out who you were and what you were about. But a car running into a house, that's a stretch.

I had my mystical side to me because my mother and her sisters Mary, Ruby, and Emma, if one of them had a dream, they would call each other and say, "I had the same dream." All of them would have these same dreams. They'd pull out their dream books and start comparing, trying to figure out what was going to happen. Between six and ten, I would also have those dreams with them. I would tell my mom, "I had a dream last night." "What was it? I had the same dream. Let's call your Aunt Mary up." I understood mysticism, or at least I had an inkling of it. That made me kind of curious about Jones, in one sense. But I couldn't really focus on that, because of all the other bullshit that outweighed it. It's like when somebody would pass a cancer, it would be stinky, but it would really be chicken guts or whatever it was. The gimmick was that you would look away because you're grossed out by it, so you don't actually see it. That was the gimmick. Okay, whatever.

There are some conflicts in that. Why would my mother lie to me? There was no reason for her to lie to me. She might have believed, but in a lot of ways she was pretty sharp. But she always let her guard down for faith healers and ministers. Those are things that happened that can't be explained. Now, I do believe in positivity, meaning that if all of us get together and meditate, or we believe in something and we truly believe it, not religiously or anything, but just like we want things to go right, we want things to be better, and we work towards that, things probably will get better. When you've got thousands of people doing that, things can happen. That's not to say that they did or didn't; I'm just saying that it can happen. It's just like when you really, really want something, and you sit there and think about it every day: "I really want this, I really want this." You meditate on it. You're not meditating like, "*Ohm*." In your mind you're going, every day, "Oh yeah, man, I want to get this new car, I want to get these glasses," whatever it might be, and you end up getting it. Then you forget about everything you did to get to that point. I thought about it every day. I didn't pray or anything, but I thought about it. I meditated. I stayed focused. I had an attitude of gratitude that it happened. Okay, well, cool. You wear your shoes, and you walk on about your business. But you also somehow made it happen. And when you have thousands of people with the same mindset, things can happen. And maybe that's where the mystical side connects with the socialist side.

Genuine socialism would be that we provide housing, we provide a safe environment, we provide food and health care. That's basic socialism. That doesn't work in America, because we charge for all those things. If you don't have enough money to pay for it, you don't get it. In a socialist society, whatever you're making, you're donating to that cause. You're giving to that cause so that everyone around you has the same as you. In Peoples Temple, in my opinion, the flaw was that there was a hierarchy. It was socialism for the minions, but for the echelon not so much. You had people who were dastardly, but they donated vociferously. They donated as much as they possibly could, so they were put into positions. They were purchasing their power. They were all on the Planning Commission. They weren't living in the Temple, in the community; they were still living in their own houses. There were other people who hadn't given up shit, weren't going to give up shit, but they followed Jones religiously. They were on PC. It was contradictory. There were doctors. There were psychologists. There were lawyers and academics. Some of them were accepted, some weren't. I don't know what the criteria were to be on PC. I know that it wasn't me. I know that some of the people on PC were on my personal list, like, "Whenever I get a chance, I'm gonna beat your ass." Like Penny Kerns, who called my mom lazy. Penny was part of PC. It made sense for Jack Beam to be on there. It made sense for Rheaviana to be on there. It even made sense for Johnny Brown or Ava Cobb to be on there because they had influence, they had impact, they were setting up for the most part a positive example for young Black men and women to follow. They had their own motivations, which might have been positive or negative. I didn't know what they were. At that time I based who my enemies were on, "Are you a hard worker or not?" If you're not a hard worker, you're an asshole.

I worked my ass off. Everybody had to work their asses off. If they weren't what I considered workers, we didn't have much in common. There were people who had specific skillsets that were necessary to the cause. When those skills were necessary, they were allowed to meander off the path, so to speak. That's not really socialism. That's modified capitalism. It's a modification that works for a lot of people, but it also hurt a lot of people. Because if you were weak you got punished, and if you were strong, you didn't. The Temple appealed to me because there was something wrong with society at large. The Temple was better than society at large. I didn't have to worry about the police coming in and jacking me up. The FBI might come in and jack me up, but the local police wouldn't. I knew that when I walked down Fillmore or Steiner or Geary, I was protected. I knew that if something happened and I was injured but not dead, there would be somebody there to fight for me, even though we didn't get along. We agreed on this: You're not going to take on one of ours. We can call them an asshole, we can call them fuckups, we can call them whatever we want to call them. You can call them whatever you want to call them, but don't you dare touch them.

For me Peoples Temple was a way of being not so much appreciated, but acknowledged for the work I did or the deeds I accomplished. There weren't any cameras, but you were always observed: your comings, your goings, what you're doing. Jack Beam relieved me of a lot of that by just allowing me to be a regular person, and to be angry when necessary. He also talked to me a lot, and said, "Everything can't be handled physically. Sometimes you're gonna have to talk your way out of it. Nobody has to like you, and you don't have to be liked by everybody. You have to know who you are and do your job. We do have a cause here. We do have a responsibility. I expect you to follow through. I'm putting you in charge of the construction crew. I'm doing that because you're a hard worker, you communicate well, and you know how to organize people. I'm gonna use your strengths."

Jack Beam was Jones's right-hand person. He was from Indiana, and he followed him out to California. Jack and his wife Rheaviana and their daughter had always been supporters of Jim Jones. Jack just really protected me, many times when I had whooped somebody's ass. On a Wednesday night, everybody yelling for my neck, Jones looking over his glasses at me like, "I've got to do something. I can't let you slide with this. You've gone too far this time," Jack would go up there and whisper in his ear. Jones would push his glasses back on his nose and say, "Okay. Well, Eugene, you know, you're a hard worker. You're responsible. Just don't make this mistake again." I'd walk off the floor. My wife would walk off the floor. I didn't get slapped. I didn't get kicked. I didn't have to fight.

I did make it known that I wasn't taking an ass-whooping publicly. I was willing to stand or die by that. I don't mind discipline, but you're not going to whoop my ass. You're not going to humiliate me. You're not going to beat me up physically. There were a couple of guys from LA that were really good fighters, and they'd just line people up until they finally weakened them. Whoop their ass. I didn't come out and just scream, like, "You're not gonna get away with this." But I made it clear that I wasn't going to take any ass-whooping. I say that not with bravado, but again, it's not what you do, it's what they think you'll do. I stood by that. By challenging hierarchy, I showed that it wasn't that I didn't have respect, but I was willing to challenge things that I thought were wrong. My homeboy Beau supported me on that. That in itself was unusual because people weren't doing that, at least as I saw it, and if they did, they were asked to leave. I wasn't asked to leave. For some reason they held onto me, and Jack supported me.

The construction crew basically dealt with rehab of houses that were donated in San Francisco for members. But the major part ended up being when the decision was made, not that we were going to Jonestown, but that we were building there. We were building the crates out in the back lot of the San Francisco Temple. We finally got the plans for the crates, and how to build them, so they could be shipped and everything. That's what we did, from seven in the morning until meeting time. The only time we stopped was when there was a meeting in the building. If there wasn't a meeting in the building, we worked well into the night.

What was interesting about Peoples Temple was that yeah, we had a construction crew, but we also had a wood shop. Harry Edwards was a plumber who was willing to teach all of us. There were people who had expertise, who shared it with us young people. They shared it with me specifically, which allowed me to run this construction crew in a rational manner. I'd look at these kids, who were the same age as I was, but I still considered them kids for whatever reason. I would find their strengths, and that's what they did. I wouldn't put them in a situation where they were weak. I put them in a situation where they were learning, but they weren't threatened by it. I always supported them. If they had an argument with somebody, I supported them. "If you're on the construction crew, I've got your back." That's how I ran the construction crew, and that was in conflict with the Jones boys and some of their crew. There were things that they worked on as well. They weren't quite, in my opinion, as sophisticated or skilled as we were. They didn't quite understand building a crew. What they did understand was keeping family and close friends together on the same team. That's much easier than creating a crew from people you don't know, and trying to find their strengths and weaknesses and then exploiting their strengths to a point where everybody feels good.

My guys walked around with their chests out, chins up, heads held high. They were proud, and I was proud of them. They always got commendations on the floor from Jones and other people. I said, "Look, I don't care how hard we're working. If you see a senior walking up that ramp, help her or him up the ramp. If you see a kid out there, make sure you grab that kid and make sure he doesn't get hurt. Tell him why you're grabbing him." I made them communicate like I would communicate. Jack Beam saw what I was doing, and he really appreciated it. I think that's why he always came to my rescue.

I was haughty, and I had no issues with that. Whoever my girlfriend was at the time, she got the same privileges that I did. You do not fuck with her. This is my friend. He gets the same privileges I do. Don't fuck with him. Some people liked that, but a lot of people didn't. I was haughty because I was better than them. What I meant by that was that I was adopted too, same as the Jones boys. I went to the Adventist Academy. I'm very educated. I fight with my mind, I fight with my mouth, and I fight with my fist. There's no weakness here. I was willing to challenge physically, damn the risk. It kept my enemies at bay and my friends very, very close.

I felt the need to fight because we were in a revolutionary group. You had to fight. Sometimes you fought the enemy, and sometimes you fought those who weren't your enemy. What I didn't get at that time was that one must temper oneself and save oneself for the battle. I didn't do that. Never tempered myself. The only time I got close to tempering myself was when Leona Collier told me, the day before I left for Guyana, "When you get there, Eugene, shut your mouth. Listen and observe." That's the only time I was tempered in Peoples Temple. And that's the only time I felt I had to be tempered, because someone I knew who was strong, who was connected, who was part of the hierarchy, who was very intelligent, very sharp, very articulate, very calculating, had told me this. And it seemed sensible. I followed that suggestion and, for right or wrong, bad or indifferent, and despite the loss of my family, because of that, I'm here. So I thank you, Leona. Leona didn't die in Jonestown. She was in San Francisco on November 18, 1978. I never made contact with her again after that.

So Peoples Temple was a conundrum, because there was hierarchy. There were favorites. There were those that were despised. There were those individuals who just couldn't rise the way that the echelon wanted them to rise. People made mistakes. It was almost as if, if you made a mistake and they embarrassed and demeaned you publicly, maybe that would teach somebody else not to do the same thing. That always irked me, from very early on. It's like, "I'm not taking an ass-whooping on stage. You're gonna have to line those people up. And when you line those people up, I'm gonna take their names and I'm gonna get them individually." I wasn't shy about that, here or overseas.

I only had a few friends in the Temple. It was a real tight group. I lost the majority of them, it seems like, when I went to Jonestown. It wasn't that I was persona non grata when I arrived. It was just that, "You're just too hot." I guess some kind of message might have been conveyed about me. There were messages conveyed all the time, and that might have been one of them. But for whatever reason, me and Eddie Crenshaw, we were tight. Bruce Oliver, tight. Joe Wilson, tight. Emmett Griffith, tight. Sebastian McMurry, tight. Sebastian was my adopted cousin. His dad was in the military, so he and his younger brother Teddy were born in Germany. Sebastian was a black belt in martial arts, and we became pretty close. He used to wear this red, black, and green Black liberation jumpsuit. Times and people change, but we stayed pretty close. I lost a lot of close friends, and adopted friends that were closer than friends: "You're gonna be my cousin. Yeah, we're this and that." That's how we introduced each other: "Oh, that's my cousin Sebastian, he's from Germany." We looked out for each other. Sebastian and Teddy both died in Jonestown.

These were my homeboys, my confidants. These were the ones that, "We're going to battle, guys." The only one of my homeboys that was on the construction crew was Beau. The rest were on different crews and doing different things. But I had my camaraderie.

What I've always learned is that you always protect yourself by surrounding yourself. It doesn't mean you always surround yourself with your best friends, or with the people who agree with you. You surround yourself with people that are like you. That's your first level of defense. If enemies get past them, then they get to people who support you but who aren't verbal about you. That's your second level of defense. The third level of defense are your homeboys. We go down together. That was me and Beau. But I had all these extensions of associates and friends that I created a barrier with. That's how I am now, to a certain extent, or at least how I was when I was working. I'm retired now. I created different levels to get to me. But I always made it a point, even in working for the State of California, to be outspoken, and not to back down. Working for a state agency, you can't get physical. But you can be verbal, and you can be intelligent, and you can be conniving, and you can be political. I took all of those on as a badge of honor, and that's what I used to survive, working for the State of California. That worked for me.

Joe Wilson had joined the Temple back east. Joe was American Indian, Chinese, and African American. Very dark. He was wearing a bald head, in the '70s, which was like, "What? You don't have an Afro?" He was a stand-alone at that time. His mother and father were very educated. He'd just gotten out, did a little bit of time. So we became cool, because he was an outcast. We went on a cross-country trip, and we came back through Seattle, and Joe and I and Thomas Johnson went to a party there after the Temple meeting. Thomas is stepping on people's toes and shoes and shit. Like, "Man, we're gonna have to fight our way out of here if you don't calm down." I was getting on edge. Thomas didn't quite grasp it, and Joe was on alert. So it was like, "Okay, man, it's time to go." And nothing happened, but Joe was really perceptive about how people were responding to us.

I say that to say this: When we got to LA, Joe said, "Hey man, you can stay with me and my relatives over here in LA." He had a cousin called Chuck, who had a '57 Chevy Bel Air. It was yellow, and for some strange reason he had headphones hanging off the old-school coat hooks on the inside. He fixed it up. It had Cragar rims, which were really popular at that time. What their family did for fun was, they would fight. The whole family. They just got in there and started boxing. I knew how to fight but I didn't know how to box, so Joe taught me how to box. Joe taught me something I'll never forget. He said, "Look, Eugene. You don't have to punch nobody in the face. You just need to punch them. You punch their arms, you punch their chest, you punch their neck, you punch their face, and if you're close enough, you bite them. You do whatever's necessary to get you out of that situation. There's no such thing as a fucking fair fight. If he's down, you don't let him up. You kick him, and you keep kicking him. You kick them until they don't move." I took him at his word.

In years after that, Joe would be on the floor, boxing the shit out of people. In the Temple, Joe ended up being one of Jones's bodyguards. He ended up getting married to Leslie Wagner, and they had a son. That's the story you read about the young lady who escaped Jonestown with the baby through the jungle. That was Joe Wilson's wife and child who did that. Joe died in the attack at the airstrip, along with Congressman Leo Ryan and several others.

The odd thing is that women came back from Guyana, and they had children after they came back, and some brought children back with them, and it seems like the male children were and are behind bars, including Jakari Wilson. I'm sad about that. I'm even sadder that I haven't visited any of them. I'm going to change that.

I can't understand why, other than that these women saw what happens when your child's not protected. The connection is when you see what happens when children aren't protected, when they're poisoned or murdered or killed, you do everything in your world to protect your child. Now, it's okay to protect a child. But sometimes, and I'm not saying in these particular cases or anything, but in other cases I've seen, when you overprotect a child, they have no defense against the system. They know what's right and they know what's wrong, but they don't know it applies to them, and they end up getting caught up in something that they weren't ready for.

The Temple was an organization within the Fillmore that had gang members from multiple cities and states, that had an attitude of "You don't fuck with us." You can come in here, you can have a great time, you can have a free meal. We'll help you out with our lawyers, we'll stand with you in the welfare line to make sure you get a fair shake, we'll make sure you get proper medical care. We'll help you out as much as we possibly can. But you don't fuck with us. That wasn't subtle. When Jones marched down to the Nation of Islam mosque—and I guess he was the first white man to go in there—I mean, that's a brazen and bold and bodacious moment. This white socialist coming down to the Black Muslims and actually having a conversation. By doing that, it put us all on the list to be watched, because the government didn't want that. The government never wants non-allying groups or revolutionaries coming together. And that was happening. We were having gang members coming in from LA. We had gang members that had come from Chicago. We had connected up with those that were in the life, so to speak, in San Francisco. We were building coalitions with groups that normally didn't get along, because we demonstrated a common purpose and we showed them a common enemy: the government. "We're not taking this shit anymore." That's what was happening. That was attractive to a lot of people, but it was also blinding, because you're willing to accept a certain level of violence internally, to offset the violence from the outside. They were both just as vicious. The only difference was that internally you didn't go to jail. But you were jailed without bars.

It didn't have to be that way. I wasn't part of the Planning Commission, and I don't know what the internal conversations were at that time, in terms of why we had to have corporal punishment. Because that's what it was: corporal punishment of teenagers, adults, men and women, old, middle-aged, and young. There'd be some compassion upon the seniors because seniors were like, "Hell, I've been here eighty years. This shit worked for me until now. I'm eighty. You're thirty-five. You got something to learn, young man." That type of thing. Occasionally you would see things through a child's eye, and that would have a dramatic effect on you. A child would see that this guy or gal has done wrong, and that they're being punished. But they're being punished in a public fashion. So to the child's eye it's like, "Well, I never want to do that, but they deserved it, because that was bad." To an adult eye it's like, "Oh, don't want that to happen to me. I'm glad he got his ass kicked and it wasn't me. I would never do that." Or, "I did that, and it could have been bad. Oh well."

When you had your members-only night, you knew that it was members only. It was like, "This ain't gonna get out." You're not going to get teased about it. If you do get teased about it, they're going to have their asses up there explaining themselves. It's strange, because in some cases you saw that it was justified, because what they had done was way overboard. But in essence it was really fucked up that you had only one individual, Jim Jones, being judge, jury, and executioner, and, based on what he said, they reacted. That was wrong.

I got busted one time for looking at *Hustler* magazine. I guess Carlotta saw me reading it, so she reported me. "Eugene's looking at a stag magazine." Whatever. It's like, "Not Eugene. Not our best worker." She's like, "Oh yeah, it was Eugene. It was him." They called me: "Eugene Smith to the floor." I was like, "Oh, what the fuck is this?" I go up there, Ollie comes up, then Carlotta comes up and says, "You were looking at *Hustler* magazine." It was almost as if she said, "Who the hell does he think he is? He's married, blah blah blah." Jones drops his glasses and looks at me, like he would always do. He says, "Tell us, Eugene, what happened?" You're not allowed to defend yourself.

"I was reading the articles," I said, and the whole crowd cracked up.

"Tell us about it," says Jones.

I told him about Jimmy Carter's brother and the beer. Then Jack Beam whispers to Jones and then says something like, "Carlotta, don't you have anything else to focus on? This man's a good worker." They turned it all the way around, and now Carlotta's on the floor, and I'm in the background with my wife saying, "Phew." Carlotta ends up getting disciplined, but it was just that she had to work harder and longer or whatever. There are situations like that where I always say you've got to read. Having read the articles, as well as looking at the pictures, saved my ass that night.

Always read. That's the moral of the story. Look at the pictures, but read the stories too.

I loved Ollie. Ollie and I went through hell together. Her mother had seen me when I was younger, just flirting with girls or whatnot, and she just didn't want that for her daughter.

The way I met Ollie was that we were on the Greyhound bus, one of the Jones buses coming back from LA, and she's up in the luggage rack, and my girlfriend at that time, Tinetra, was in the luggage rack with her. Ollie said, "If you're getting off at Fresno, we're going back to the Bay Area. You want to hop up here so you can be with Tinetra?" She was like fourteen then. I said, "Sure, thank you." I get off the bus in Fresno, and after that Ollie and I were friends, and I knew her brother and her older sisters. Her older sisters hung out with one of my best friends, my cousin, Sebastian. Then, when I moved up to San Francisco two years later, Ollie and I would see each other and we'd talk. I had broken up with Tinetra. I wasn't with anybody, and we'd just talk. Just walk and talk. We'd walk over to Golden Gate Park or go down to the beach. It was dangerous taking her to the beach, because she had a disease, but I forget what it's called. She's at the beach, and the ocean's going, and the waves are coming in, and she would just walk right into it, almost like a hypnosis, and you couldn't stop her. I had to stay up on the sea wall, rather than go down to the beach. Then we started dating, and her mom found out, and her mom beat her with a telephone cord. Ollie ran away and came to the Temple, and I met her at the front door.

"What's wrong?"

"My mom beat me." She had these welts all over her.

I went to Anita Ijames and said, "Hey, I can't take this. She's getting beat for seeing me. That's not right." Ollie's mother called and said, "I'm coming to get my daughter tomorrow. She better be ready." Her mom came in the front door the next day, and I told her, "Don't you ever beat her again. You beat her again, I'll fucking kill you." So she beat her again, just to make a fucking point of it.

I contacted Mike Prokes, the Temple spokesman. The attorneys ran it past Jones and came back down and said, "Hey, the only way y'all can get out of this is, you have to go to Arkansas. She's sixteen, you're eighteen.

You can get married there, but you can't get married here. Now remember, if you don't get married, you can't come back here, because you're crossing state lines with a minor, and that's statutory rape." Ollie and I talked about it, and we cried, and then we said, "Okay. We'll do it." We got on the bus at the Greyhound station in Oakland. Ruby Carroll and Anita Ijames drove us over there and dropped us off. They said, "Hey, next time we see you guys, you're gonna be husband and wife. Be careful." They gave us a little bit of spending money, and we caught the bus to Little Rock, Arkansas.

Our first night there we check into a hotel and go up to this room, and somebody's been putting out cigarettes on the wall, on the blanket and everything, just a trashy fucking room. I go downstairs and go off about living in a fucking pig sty. Then we get a decent room, and the next morning we get breakfast in and try to find out how we're going to get married. We go down to city hall. They say, "Oh no, we've got to have a parent sign for this. Or your legal guardian." So we call back to the attorneys at the Temple in San Francisco and say, "Hey, this is not happening." They say, "It has to happen. Her mom is freaking out. You've been charged with kidnapping. You've got to marry her. You better figure out a way." We go around, and we're trying to figure out what we can do. So now we're three days into it. We're walking at night and we come upon a Klan meeting, which is not unusual in Little Rock, Arkansas. We're looking at it through the fence and I say, "We got to get out of here before we fucking get strung up or something." We go back to the hotel room. Now we're running out of cash.

A few days later, the last day, we're down to like twenty dollars. We're sitting at the bus stop, and we get into an argument because we're just stressed. Last day in a hotel, because we don't have any more money for that. And I said, "Let me try this couple across the street." So I walk across the street and there's this guy, and he's from Africa. I don't know which country in Africa. I explain the situation and say, "Hey man, I can't go back to California because my girlfriend is underage and I'm gonna be on the run for the rest of my life, or at least for the next two years until she turns eighteen, if I don't marry her." He says, "Man, I'm here on the Green Card. I can't help you. My girlfriend will be out here in a moment, talk to her." The girl comes out and I explain it to her, and she says, real matter of fact, "Do you love her?"

I said, "Yes."

"Okay, I'll sign for you," she says.

"Well, what do I owe you?"

"You don't owe me anything. I understand this."

So she goes over to city hall with us, justice of the peace, and she signs. We get married and we just start crying, because it's like finally something broke that was correct. We get married, then we catch the bus to Des Moines, Iowa, because Jones is on a cross-country trip, and we catch up with him there. And we returned to California as a married couple.

Ollie's mother wouldn't speak to her for a while. Her brother Marvin and her sisters would speak to her, but they didn't really communicate with me. Then they started talking to me finally, but her mother never would. Then, when she found out Ollie was pregnant, it was basically too late, because Ollie was leaving the country in a few weeks. That was two years later. Ollie was eighteen then, in 1978, and I was twenty. Her mom basically had just cut her off. Ollie's mom was a member of the Temple. Her grandmother was over there, in Guyana. I didn't really know her that well. My mom quit speaking to me, because I hadn't told her that I was getting married. She took it real personal. But once the baby arrived, "Oh, he looks just like you," and all that kind of stuff. We ended on a decent relationship. That was a good thing.

CHAPTER 5
Welcome to Jonestown

I'm in San Francisco, it's the end of February 1978, and my number finally pops up for me to leave for Jonestown. We're going to be the largest contingent leaving, a hundred-plus people. Previous groups flew to Miami and from there to Guyana, but we're going to take the bus all the way across the country, because now the Concerned Relatives are watching all the airports on the West Coast. We load the bus up at the San Francisco Temple, in the rear. We load up all our gear and stuff to be taken over: materiel, medicines, and other things that need to be delivered to people in Jonestown. Many of us on the bus are the LA-based construction crew led by Archie Ijames. The rest of the San Francisco crew that I led are already in Jonestown, and I've been transferred to the LA crew. I don't remember Archie being on the bus with us, but I remember some other crew members, like Kenny Wilhite, Jerry Rhea, and Jerome Simon.

It's a few days going across. We slept on the bus and everything. It's exciting, but it's also wrenching, because I know I'm not coming back. It's like I'm saying goodbye not only to the Temple, but to the United States. I'm not coming back. It was not my intention to return here ever again. And most of us were in that mindset, but happy to be leaving. People are getting agitated. People are happy. People are excited. The whole gamut of personality traits and attitudes are rearing their heads on that bus. And there are seniors. I think we were in two buses. Stopping at rest stops in Texas and stuff like that. We had our own food and everything. And we're sightseeing at the same time. But nobody took pictures. There were multiple cameras, but nobody took pictures, because we were so in the moment, so to speak. "I don't want to document this; I just want to leave."

I think we got to Miami at night, and we left the next morning. I'm twenty years old, and I've never been on an airplane before. Been in the airport dozens, if not hundreds, of times, taking other members to the airports to leave. But I'd never been on a plane. I didn't see that as either an asset or a deficit. I'd just never been on an airplane before. It never interested me. Never been to Miami either. I'd been to multiple states, but not to Florida. I was born in Detroit, then went to Chicago. And then Arkansas, Los Angeles, Fresno, San Francisco, Richmond. My life was on the West Coast. And back to Arkansas a couple times for family reunions as a kid and then to get married, but that was the extent of it. And back to Detroit once; I must've been nineteen. Went back with Peoples Temple, when they were going on a cross-country tour. Stopped in Detroit.

So I get on the airplane. Now, I'm excited. I'm not afraid, because I don't think we're going to get hijacked. If you can remember back, airplanes were getting hijacked to Cuba pretty regularly in the '70s. But I figured nobody wanted us, so it was no big issue. So we're on the plane, and we're the majority of the people on the plane. It's not a private plane or anything, but it's just us. And we're laughing and talking and everything. Then I'm thinking back like, "Wow, I'll never see this again. I'll never be in the US again. I'll never see San Francisco. I'll never see Fresno. I'll never see LA. I'll never see my cousins. The people I went to elementary school and high school with, I'll never see them again." But I'm okay with that.

The stopover is in Port of Spain, Trinidad. I think it was maybe a four- or five-hour stopover, maybe more than that. I get off the plane and walk across the tarmac into the terminal. And I see these Black women. They're chocolate. They're cocoa. They're mocha. They're cream. Every incarnation of Black women I could imagine. They've got Afros. Yeah, this is heaven. I'd never seen this many beautiful Black women in one place. And then I look around. After I get past the Black women, it's like the whole airport is Black. Oh, this is great! The white people are looking around like we usually look around: "Is there another one? Is there another white person around here?" So I'm laughing. I'm cracking up, because it's interesting to see white people in a position where they're the minority. And they're looking for another one of themselves, and they can't find any. It's like, yes! This is cool. And Guyana's Black, too. This is really going to be interesting. And so we sit there, and I'm just gawking. I'm seeing people in every position there was at the airport, and they are Black. Which I had never seen in the US.

When we land in Georgetown, it's daytime. And as soon as we get off the plane at the airport, someone said, "Come on through. Everybody give me your passports." So we gave them our passports. They walked our passports through and just told us, "Go, go, go, go." No check, no nothing. Just "Go, go, go." It was somebody from the Lamaha Gardens house, probably Patricia Cartmell, daughter of Patty Cartmell, who ran the boat up the Kaituma River and was one of Jones's most trusted aides. And they were in with the customs. "It's Peoples Temple, don't worry, just walk on through." So it's like, "Yeah, yeah. That's right. Respect me. Respect me." We get out there and, "We'll get your luggage. You guys all get in the van." They had vans and trucks. And the truck was the Bedford, which I loved. It had the high rails on it. They're putting all the luggage back there. We helped them load it up.

And we get in the vans and start driving into Georgetown. We're going through jungle that's been cut back, and we're going past villages, and I'm seeing poverty now. I realize I'm in a Third World country. All that elation is now tempered, because I'm seeing lean-tos on the side of the road, where people are living. I'd been to Mexico, but it wasn't poverty like this. They have little fruit stands or juice stands or whatnot. I don't remember seeing people begging or anything. But it was my first case, and my last case, of seeing someone with elephantiasis. That shocked me. But it slapped me back to reality, that this wasn't going to be the journey that I thought it was going to be.

Then we get into Georgetown. We're off a red clay road and onto pavement, and we're going to Lamaha Gardens. You hear the name Lamaha Gardens, and you're expecting an estate. It's not an estate. But for Guyana it was, in comparison to what was surrounding us. And I see there's a big canal in front of the house. And everybody comes down and hugs us. We're all in there, crowded and everything. Some people were staying there, other people were staying at other locations. So we're on the floor, we're outside, we're on the balcony, we're in the living room. There are sleeping bags everywhere. But you didn't need a sleeping bag, because it was hot, day and night. All you needed was a sheet. That's not new, because Fresno was hot like that, although it wasn't humid. So I'm swatting off the mosquitoes. I've always had this thing about mosquitoes. My Vitamin B deficiency makes me really sweet to them. And they said we'd be there one to two weeks, just to acclimate before we get into the bush, because the bush was going to be much worse.

So we're riding around town, and they've already confiscated all our passports and stuff. But I kept my driver's license, and I kept my Social Security card. I don't remember them asking for those, but I remember a lot of people didn't have them when they returned. And I was there such a short length of time that my driver's license didn't even expire. In the house, we're not hearing any preaching or anything. Occasionally, they had a radio room downstairs. And someone would say, "Father's on the line right now. Come on down." So those of the echelon would go down and listen to whatever they listened to. And on Sunday evenings you would hear music. I think it was the Atlantic Steel Drum Orchestra; they were across the way from us. They were a constant on Sundays, which was just fantastic, because a steel drum can sound like any instrument you want it to sound like. It's live, and they're practicing. Just fantastic. So we're touring the city, and we see the estate where the prime minister's at. It's like a mile and a half, two miles from the house. You could see parts of the zoo and whatnot. And that was nice. And it's not like the elation returned, but the comfort returned: "Okay, this can be all right."

And then some people leave for Jonestown. I was at Lamaha Gardens a couple of weeks. And finally they said, "Okay, we're gonna be leaving in a couple days. Start organizing your stuff." And we went down to the dock, it seems like two days before, because we were putting ice in the hull of the *Cudjoe*, also known as the *Marceline*, the boat we were going to take to Port Kaituma. And they were bringing on these huge hammerhead sharks. That's what we're going to eat on the way down. We had shark burgers. You scrape the skin, make a patty, and you've got a burger. That was exciting. So we leave out of Georgetown on the *Cudjoe*. It was decided that the seniors would sleep below at night, rather than sleeping on deck, because we'll be hitting waves. And I'm thinking, "No big thing." I didn't realize the waves were going to be cresting over the boat. Because the Atlantic Ocean is up and down, up and down, whereas the Pacific is like a swoon. The Pacific flows like a wave would. The Atlantic comes to the top and just drops down drastically. And that's what the boat was doing. And when the boat would drop, the wave would come across the bow. This is the open ocean. We didn't go along the shoreline. In some places I couldn't even see the shoreline. It took twenty-four hours to get to Jonestown from Georgetown. Probably fourteen to sixteen hours on the ocean, then eight hours going up the Kaituma River.

So we wake up the next morning, not that I had slept that night; my eyes are sore because I've been wide-eyed all night. Like, "What the fuck is this? There's a fucking wave over there. Are we gonna make it?" But we finally get into calm water. The water goes from the murky green of the Atlantic to the muddy brown of the Kaituma River. I'd already been to the library and studied on the river. I knew there were caimans and freshwater otters. There were also piranha. But I knew there were over ninety species of piranha; I just didn't know which species this was. Everybody is sweltering. We've eaten. You can only eat so much on a boat. And there's no shade. You're just fucking sweltering. So when we get into calm water, Jerry Rhea and Jerome jump into the water. And everybody's saying, "Piranha! Piranha!" But what we forgot was that if you don't have any mosquito bites, no blood or anything, you're okay. They're not going to mess with you. Piranhas are attracted to blood or open sores or bumps. But it got everybody's attention that this ain't Lake Mendocino. This ain't Clear Lake or anything like that. This is untamed river.

By the time we get into the small village of Port Kaituma it's dark, and it's raining buckets. Now I'm cool, but I'm drenched wet. We didn't stay the night in Port Kaituma. We left that night. I forget how many miles it is from Port Kaituma, but it's like three miles just from the front gate of Jonestown to the pavilion. We're riding in the back of these hay trailers, behind these Massey Ferguson tractors. The tractors are pulling the trailers. The road is sunken, and it's red clay. There were no brakes on the tractors, because the mud was so viscous, and the water was so deep, that if you just took your foot off the gas, you would stop. The grit inside the soil just tears up the brakes anyway. So brakes were of no use, because you would be replacing them weekly. So we're riding, and we're hitting potholes the size of Volkswagens. And people are going, "Oh! Oh! Oh! Oh!" They're trying to be brave, but it scares the hell out of them, because all you can see in the dark is what's in front of that beam on the front of the tractor. It's night in rural Guyana, in the bush. There are no streetlights. There are no markers on the road, because the road is clay. And it's so dark you can't see the jungle, even though the jungle is only thirty yards away. It must have been seven or eight in the evening. I think by the time we got to the pavilion it was ten. After about an hour or so, you could see this white glow way off in the distance. You know it's Jonestown; you just don't know it's the pavilion. And then you start hearing these faint cries. But it's not cries, it's people celebrating. They're celebrating us coming. Now your adrenaline starts to flow. I'm feeling it now. Yeah, this is cool. This is cool.

The seniors must have been in the first trailer, like a half hour ahead of us. You could hear this hoopla go up. We're still down the road. And now you can see that the glow is no longer in the distance; it's right over there. But you can't get to it. So we come around the curve. And when you come into Jonestown, on the right side you had the kitchen facilities where you came in at, and then Mr. Muggs's cage further down. Mr. Muggs was a chimpanzee that Jones had adopted from an animal shelter in the States. And I remember taking off my boots and just jumping in the mud and saying, "I have arrived. I am here."

And I stomp on to the pavilion, and I'm really elated. I see Ollie. She's lost a lot of weight, but she looks good, and she's seven-plus months pregnant. I hadn't seen her in six months or so. I hadn't seen my mother in over a year. And there are people there that I hadn't seen for a couple of years. Beau, my best friend, had gone over before me; he was a driver on the tractor I was on. He'd been there three or four months already. Beau was on the basketball team. He was in Georgetown with us after November 18.

So I get there. Ollie's there. I'm hugging her. I'm hugging my mom. I'm seeing people I haven't seen. Children that were babies or infants or toddlers when they left, and now they're walking, they're talking. And it's just exciting. Everybody is celebrating, and the music is playing. And it starts dying down. And as it's dying down, Jones is calling out names. Jerry Rhea. Kenny Wilhite. Jerome Simon. Brian Bouquet, who played the saxophone in the band. Kenny and Jerry were also in the band. Jerry played the bass, and Kenny played either rhythm or lead guitar.

So Jones calls them up to the floor. He's like, "Hey, we hear you're trying to have relationships." And they start in on them. And I'm holding Ollie's hand, and I'm gripping it now, because I know this disciplinary shit is fixing to start. I haven't been here a fucking hour yet, and it's already piped up. And, before he gets to them, Jones says, "I want to let you know that we know there's spies among you. And we know that the spies are passing information via cassette tapes. So we're gonna confiscate all your cassette tapes." Well, I had 365 tapes, for every day I was going to be there for the next year, that ranged from thirty minutes to two hours each. And taking my music was like taking my soul. But they had all the luggage and everything. There was nothing I could do. So they took my tapes. Everybody that knew me knew that music was my passion. "Don't fuck with his music. You can mess with him, but don't mess with his music." They messed with my music. I was fucking mad.

And then Jones starts in on them. As he calls Kenny, Kenny's wife Cheryl runs up with his little girl, Janilah. Then he calls up Jerry Rhea. Jerry and his wife Pat have one child, Asha, and Pat is pregnant. "And you're trying to screw some other women, Mr. Rhea?" And to both Jerry and Kenny, Jones says, "You're asses. You have women here that support you in a socialist environment. We're trying to create something. And you're in Georgetown. You're coming across country on a bus, and you're fucking up. And you, Jerome. You weren't even supposed to leave the goddamn country, because you have a communicable disease. And we got you out of the country. And you're trying to screw Guyanese girls?" So then it starts with, "What are we gonna do with them?" And the first thing Jones had said when he left the US was, "We're not gonna be doing this in Jonestown. It's not necessary to do this in Jonestown. We don't need that sort of discipline in Jonestown."

Then they give us a warning. The warning is that Larry Layton is inside a box in the banana cellar, below ground but open on both sides. "Don't say anything when you go by him. Tom Grubbs is the only person supposed to talk to him." What's interesting about that is that Tom Grubbs is the only one that can talk to Larry, and Tom Grubbs is also the teacher of the children. So it looks like behavior modification: You only hear my voice and what I say.

Ollie asks me to let her hand go, because I'm gripping it too tight. I say, "I'm sorry." And then I realize that all I've got is a fucking knife. Something's definitely amiss, and all I have is a pocketknife. I know the jungle is there, but just to go through a hundred yards of jungle would take a few hours, especially if there's no trail there. It's dark in the daytime in the jungle, so going through it at night is unheard of. Fuck getting to the jungle. I can't even see the jungle to get to it. Ollie can't go. I'm looking at my mother, and she's glazed. I'm looking around, and people are applauding, and they're happy, and they're joyful. They're talking for a while about kicking these guys' asses. So then they do.

And then all of a sudden, they declare a White Night. "We're under attack. The enemy is out there. They're listening to us. Make a joyful noise." I was like, "What the fuck?" All I've got is a fucking knife. And Ollie can't go anywhere. My mother's glazed over. And Beau doesn't say shit to me.

I'm happy to see my wife. But she can't run. I'm happy to see my mother. But she won't run. I'm happy to be here. But I want to run. But running is not an option. My best friend, Beau, doesn't say shit to me, other than, "Hey, what's up?" So something's up. We're under a White Night? What the fuck is a White Night? When a White Night was called, that meant everyone had to report to the pavilion. The pavilion was where we assembled to organize, defend, or offend. When a White Night was called, you were expected to be there. If you weren't there, unless you were on the *Cudjoe* or on guard duty, you would be made an example of or treated as an enemy. I don't remember having White Nights in the US. My first White Night was my first night in Jonestown.

And I don't know why it's called a White Night. I don't know if that's a nod to the Klan, or what. (Later I was told that Jones was trying to flip around the negative connotations around the word "black," because most of us were Black. So blackmail became whitemail; the black market was called the white market.) I don't know. I do know that I'm in a pickle, and the enemy is at the door, and there's nothing I can do. Now the guards, the basketball team, Jones's entourage, they're all running around. They've got their rifles or whatnot. I'm saying, "Fuck, they don't know nothing about fucking guns." Okay, whatever. Hopefully nothing bad happens. We must've stayed up until two or three that next morning. And Jones makes this proclamation: "Well, we've got work to do, people. We can't stop because we were up all night, and we're under attack. Do you guys want to sleep in, or do you want to go to work at your regular time?" The seniors raise their hands: "No, we don't need to sleep in." And the children say no. And those in the middle just say no. And I'm like, "Fuck. I need to sleep in." But you can't say that.

And Jones says, "Okay. Walk people to their cottages. We'll be getting up at the regular time." At six o'clock or something. "And we'll start our regular work day tomorrow." Welcome to Jonestown, so to speak.

So I'm walking with Ollie, and we're going to this cottage. The cottages are really small, and it was like four couples on the bottom, and two couples up top, something like that. Just a lot of people. And no windows. Spaces cut in the walls where you can lift out the flap, but no glass or screen windows. I learned later that they would take termite hills and cut the tops of them off and put them underneath the huts and light them up. Those fumes would chase all the mosquitoes away. So I didn't get ate up that night. But over the next couple weeks I got ate up, which is how I got yellow fever or malaria, or whatever it was that I got. I was in ICU when my baby was being delivered. I believe it was malaria, but I'm not really sure. I just know that I lost twenty-five pounds in five days. And I just shit, shit, shit. Some people said malaria, other people said yellow fever. So I just said yellow malaria. And the outhouse is a hundred yards away. It's like, I'm holding this until morning. I'm not walking out there. And I'm sitting there, and I'm laying next to Ollie. And I'm just, "What have I got myself into?" Ollie seems truly okay. She seems safe. She's a bit smaller, but everybody is smaller, but not in an unhealthy sense. Just smaller. I mean, all the baby fat, and all the chemicals, are out of their bodies. They look healthy.

So we get up the next morning, and everybody's supposed to do thirty days work in the field right after arriving. I remember Mark Cordell was one of the guards. I considered him one of the Jones boys, because of his close relationship with Stephan and Jimmy. When they were around he had only a little bravado, and stateside he was a lazy fucker. And now he's lording over me. No way. I remember thinking: "Twentieth-century slaves." But everybody does it. It's thirty days. I'll deal with it. But as soon as I get past the thirty-first fucking day, there's gonna be some reckoning. My very first day we were cutting all the underbrush out so they could make a windrow, burn that, and start clearing out the land and grading it so we could plant vegetables. I'm on the edge of the bush, and Bob Rankin, who had previously been on the construction crew in LA, says to me: "Just freeze. Just stop. Don't move." Bob was probably in his late thirties. And then I hear this *whoosh*. Bob is cutting the head off a viper that's right in the vines in front of me, bobbing its head, within striking distance. Because I haven't become color conscious of the different variations of green, I didn't see it. It was camouflaged. But Bob Rankin saw it and saved me. I'm grateful and indebted to him. Bob died on November 18.

I made it those first few days of that first week, but the mosquitoes just ate me fucking alive. That's when I got sick and they put me in ICU. I was in there a week. And then Ollie went into labor.

I said, "I want to see."

They said, "No, Eugene, you can't go."

"Please help me."

So Julie Flowers, one of the nurses, helped me out. I got there, and I could see his curly hair coming out. And I fainted. So they hold me up and take me outside. I say, "I'm okay. I'm all right now. I got some fresh air. It's just a fever." So I go back in, and I see my baby delivered. And I didn't notice the umbilical cord. I go back in the ICU. Ollie's okay, the baby's okay. And then Jones announces that night that there was an umbilical cord around my baby's neck, and thanks to him the baby was saved, blah blah blah. But I don't remember seeing an umbilical cord. Jones always took credit. Not for everything, but for most stuff.

So I'm still in ICU, and Ollie brings the baby to the window every day. I don't know how long I was in there. Finally, I get out. But when I get out, I don't get put back in the field. I go to the shoe shop with Chuck Beikman, and now I'm repairing and making shoes and repairing boots and stuff.

Jones is on the loudspeaker on a daily basis. Ollie and I and the baby have now moved out of the hut, and we're living in the nursery. So we've got a regular-sized bed, and we have some privacy. The baby is healthy. Things are comfortable. I don't remember there being any White Nights for those few weeks or whatever. But I get tired of hearing only the BBC and Jones on the radio. So I say, "I want to be on the wood crew." You don't transfer yourself over there. You don't make decisions yourself about where you're going to go. But I did, because that's what I was accustomed to. So I was now on the wood crew, and I was able to venture much further out. Yeah, I worked hard, but it was exciting. It was a rush. I got to see some of the wildlife. Every now and again we ran across a local Amerindian. They'd be passing through doing their thing, and we're doing ours. Have a little wave that says, like seeing somebody on the street, "Hey, how you doin'?" Just keep going. When we broke our ax handles, the Amerindians showed us how to make one out of a sapling. "Here, you can make your ax handle right here. Don't worry about it." We walked through the jungle with rain boots. They walked through barefooted. It's their jungle. That was good, being out in nature, out in the jungle. That's when I really fell in love with it, because it was a retreat from the heat. The jungle was unforgiving. Everything beautiful was dangerous. You see the yellow and black frogs, the red and yellow frogs, the green and lime green frogs. They were poison. But the Amerindians understood that. Certain poisons: "Oh, we're gonna hunt monkeys with that. It relaxes all their muscles, so they don't grab anything and just fall out of the tree." They had all these different poisons for different animals they were hunting.

I knew I wasn't coming back to the US. And I wasn't sad about that. I was kind of relieved. Because now I'm out of this shit, and I can look back at it. At that time, that's how I felt. I'm leaving this shithole, and I'm going to Jonestown. I was done. And the thing is, I didn't have any illusions about Jonestown. I knew it was going to be primitive. Before leaving I lived in the Temple in San Francisco and with Leona Collier, who said, the day before my group left, "Eugene, when you get to Jonestown, shut your mouth. Don't say nothing. Just listen. If you're in trouble, I'm gonna be there probably in the next couple of months. I will get you and Ollie out. But don't say anything. Just observe." And that's what I did—with the exception of saying that I wanted to be on the wood crew.

I was privileged. In California I was in charge of the construction crew. I didn't get disciplined. I had fights on a regular basis, but I did not get disciplined. Ollie didn't get disciplined. I did what I wanted to do. I told Leona where I wanted to go and how I wanted to get there. And I didn't take advantage of that situation, but I did use it to my benefit, to get done what I needed to do, or what made me feel comfortable.

I didn't anticipate that I was going into an abusive environment in Jonestown. When Leona told me what she told me, it was because I was very outspoken. And since nobody was there to challenge me, she was like, "Don't take that attitude with you. Shut up and sit down and listen." She was giving me motherly advice: "Just listen and observe." It wasn't like, "You're going into danger," but rather, "Just listen and observe. Be smart about this, Eugene. You won't be in the United States anymore. And everybody you crossed here is gonna be there. All the fights you won here, the losers are gonna be there."

I was not ready for the White Night. And that's why I grabbed Ollie's hand, and why I grabbed my knife. And after that I was on alert. That was a turning point. If your best friend is not communicating with you, and you're in a hostile environment, you're obviously in enemy territory. You have no reason not to be on alert. I had a wife and a child. And Ollie had

Christa. Christa was Sharon Amos's daughter, and she saw Ollie as her mother, rather than Sharon Amos. So if Ollie accepts Christa, I accept her. And if we run, we all run together.

But there was nowhere to run to, because I didn't know where to run to. I had to find some way to get into the bush, and that was the wood crew. I've got to learn these routes, these trails. And even after learning that, it's like, Christa would be okay, but Ollie with a newborn wouldn't. So I shut my mouth. I listened. I observed. But that first night I was like, "Fuck this. I'm not putting up with this." I accepted the shit in the US, with the illusion that we didn't want our young men and women in jail in the capitalist system, we would handle it ourselves. We won't share our dirty laundry. Well, fuck. We're in the jungle now. What's the purpose of this? You've got a guy, Larry Layton, in a fucking box below ground. You're beating people for having inappropriate relationships. We're having White Nights. And I'm hearing Leona's voice saying, "Just shut your mouth, listen, and observe."

I was never touched. Ollie was never touched. Our baby was never touched. Well they were, in the end. But up until that point, there was no disciplinary action on them or anything. Ollie had a temper, and she was outspoken. Here she was in a position to be outspoken, because she was protected. But when Leona got there, she knew I was in trouble, but I couldn't tell her. And she knew I wasn't going to leave Ollie. It was a catch-22. I don't know what torment she might've gone through, in terms of, "I want to save Eugene, and leave Ollie." Or, "I want to save Ollie and leave Eugene." I don't know what Leona's torment was, but I'm sure it was torment, because I could see it on her face.

See, here's the thing. Promises were made: "We're gonna go to Jonestown. Guyana is a socialist country. We'll be able to farm. We'll be left alone. We'll handle our own problems. We won't have to do this corporal punishment. The only reason we're doing corporal punishment is because we don't want these men and women to go to jail here in the US. We have corporal punishment, we handle our own." In Jonestown that wouldn't be necessary, said Jones, because we would be in a different environment, and there would be no reason for it.

Within an hour of my arrival, that was shit on the wall.

I have to keep flashing back because I have to bring you into it, because it's like, "He said this, but what does it mean?" I have to give you all of that as well. The issue with trying to write my story is that I'm constantly having to go back to bring people up to speed. Otherwise, it doesn't connect.

Our son Martin was born several weeks after I arrived. People think he was named after Martin Luther King, but actually it was Martin so that Christa Amos could have a baby brother, in lieu of her own brother Martin. Christa wanted a brother that she could take care of. I said, "Fine, his name is Martin." He was born on June 7, 1978. I had to look up that date for this book, because that's definitely something I blanked out of my mind. I blanked both Martin's birthday and Ollie's birthday—November 6, 1959—out of my mind. I didn't want to remember their birthdays. I know what day they died; that's more than enough. I can't justify it, but I tell people, "If you want to feel bad, forget the day your child was born. It's supposed to be the most beautiful moment there is, but it wasn't." It was beautiful that he was born, but he died only a few months later, and it wasn't because of disease or anything, but because somebody made a choice. I only got to bond with him for maybe six weeks before I went to Georgetown. I wasn't able to build a relationship. I mean, you build a relationship, but when you've got paranoia going on, you've got constant White Nights going on, you think you're under attack, you think this is going to be your last day on earth, you savor the moment, but there are things that aren't as important. It doesn't matter what day he was born; he was here. It doesn't matter what day Ollie was born; she was here. But now they're both gone. All I remember is the day they died.

I was in Jonestown a little more than five months, then I was in Georgetown for maybe three and a half months. In Jonestown I remember finding land tortoises, I remember finding sloths. I remember listening to the howler monkeys at night; they sound like the wind blowing. There are some good memories there, but they're eclipsed by the tragedy. I tell people there were moments of absolute joy that were overwhelmed by just seconds of ultimate tragedy, and war almost, within the community. And there were challenges that got shot down. Jones would say something and people would say, "We don't agree with that." He'd say, "You're not faithful! You're not faithful! You should follow the cause!" All that kind of stuff. People changed. People that I was friends with here, I wasn't friends with there, because we had different mindsets. They'd been indoctrinated. They'd been there to a point where there was no out for them. For whatever reason, I had an out. I had always had an out. I just didn't know it, and I didn't know why. There were plenty of times that I did things, that other people did the same thing, but they got all kinds of penalties and corporal punishment, and I just walked away from it.

I'll give you a perfect instance. I'd been in Jonestown a week or so, and there's a person, he's called on the floor during a meeting, and his children testify against him: "Daddy was a jerk," whatever. And he gets disciplined for it. What do you do with that? You don't trust your children? Or in reverse, you turn your child in for doing something. You don't trust your parents? No one trusts anybody, so therefore you're all walking around with fear in your hearts, all trying to figure it out, but nobody has anybody to bounce it off of. It's just you talking to yourself. Even though you're in the midst of a jungle, there's no solitude, because you're in this village of a thousand people, and it never goes to sleep, because there's guards up at night, there's people walking around checking out things. It takes an effort to adapt to quiet, when you're coming from an environment such as San Francisco.

And you're going to an environment where you hear, "Ah," and it's not the wind. It's the howler monkey. Or you hear the squeal occasionally. The macaws wake you up in the morning when they fly. They fly into the bush in the daytime, and they fly out of the bush at night. They'd be in large trees so they can watch the surroundings. You've got fruit bats that have a wingspan of a foot and a half, two feet. You have frogs that have skin and secretions that are toxic to you. You have plants that are toxic to you. They won't kill you, but they'll just make you really miserable. You don't have the resources that you would have in a city. When you're out in the bush, you don't have toilet tissue. So you've got to use what's called a cow leaf. But if you don't wash that cow leaf first, all these little mites and stuff get on you, and we used to have what was called the Jonestown itch. It would be like athlete's foot in your crotch or your butt or something.

There were things to be dealt with. The food environment was much different. I barely remember breakfast, but I remember that every day for dinner it was rice and something. Lots of rice. I don't have any issue with that. It didn't affect me negatively, but for some people it did, because they expected a different environment. They expected it to be the promised land, and it was everything but the promised land. The promise was what you got here. There was always something happening. But you're supposed to ignore Larry Layton in a box in the banana cellar underground, because "I've labeled him, me, Jim Jones, I have labeled him a spy, or less than desirable." And it became Jones's law, not the people's law. And it was just as bad as being back in San Francisco. Wednesday nights in San Francisco, members' night, would be catharsis. Well, the same thing happened in Jonestown, except it wasn't just on Wednesday nights. It could be any night.

And that first night, after my group arrived, was a White Night. So we stayed up until like four o'clock in the morning, making noise so we wouldn't be attacked, but you're still expected to get up at six. What they said that night was, "Well, do you guys want to sleep in? Or do you want to get up for the cause?" All the seniors said, "Well, I want to get up for the cause because I'm only gonna be in the kitchen. I'm not gonna be in the field." And this is no slur against the seniors. It just is what it is. And I have no malice or anger towards them for that, because they shouldn't have had to work. They worked hard for sixty years before they got there. But it made it difficult.

So that created a little chasm. You had all these separate little chasms happening, these little cracks in the woodwork. Wives turned in husbands, husbands turned in wives, for misdeeds of some type. "Heard you say something that was negative toward the cause. Heard you were planning to get away." And Jones says, "You know, there's 250 miles of jungle out there. If it takes you twenty-four hours by boat, imagine what it'd take you trying to trek through that jungle." He also claimed the police in Port Kaituma would turn us over to him, or that Guyanese and US government officials in Georgetown would return us to Jonestown. So people, even though they might have wanted to leave, might have thought about leaving, even planned to leave, were frightened by him saying things like that: "You're not gonna make it." And a lot of it was ballyhoo. Rubble, rubbish. But the essence of it was that it was a very dangerous jungle.

Jones's mother passed away, and they wanted to get her out of the camp surreptitiously. People die, and she was very much up in age. But I remember hearing that there might have been a feeling that people would have lost faith in Jones, because his mother died. Supposedly there were miracles done in Jonestown, but he wasn't doing faith healings like he had been doing in California. Like when my son Martin was born and Jones was all, "Oh, there was an umbilical cord around his neck, and I blah blah blah saved your son." Okay, well, you know, one way or another, even though Julie Flowers and other nurses and doctors were there, but okay, fine, you can have that one.

But anyway, they brought out Jones's mother and we had to bury her. At least I was told the woman we were burying was Jones's mother. I was instructed not to tell anyone. Records show that Lynetta Jones actually died in December 1977, before I arrived in Jonestown. And it makes sense now that it might not have been her that I helped bury. Had I spread the rumor that I had helped bury Jim Jones's mother, I would have been labeled and shunned as an enemy. I was the newest person on the crew; everyone else there had been in Jonestown for at least six months.

Most likely, according to what is known, the woman we buried that day was Chlotile Butler, who died of natural causes on June 10, 1978. Whoever it was, we took her past the pig farm and the chickery, and they wanted us to bury her further off the road so she wouldn't be found. They didn't want anybody happening upon her. It was myself, I think Eddie Crenshaw, Beau—I think Beau was the tractor driver, with Eddie assisting. We start to try to bury her. And anybody that's been in the jungle understands that there is no soil. It's just vines that cross each other. So it took forever and a day, well over ten or twelve hours, to get her buried sufficiently, because we had to break through the vines and all that kind of stuff. We might have had a backhoe out there. But even with a backhoe, we had to cut our way in there, then create an area so we could all get in there comfortably. And then break through the vines, then start digging to put her into the ground. And then we got stuck out there because it turned dark on us, and we were already in the bush. It was dark already, but now it's black.

But we get her buried. There's no ceremony or nothing. We had become responsible to bury her because she had been starting to swell up. The body was decomposing because of the heat and humidity. So it was like, "We gotta get you in the ground because there's gonna be animals coming in a little bit." It couldn't be in the compound; it had to be in the jungle. There was no place to bury in the compound, because that would contaminate the local water. There were physical reasons you couldn't bury a body near a population, because the water sources were so shallow, and there was no real way to trace where they came from or went. There were little streams and stuff everywhere. So anyway, we get her buried and we're told never to talk about it. So we never talked about it. I mean, I'm talking about it now, but I didn't talk about it then.

I loved the jungle because it was security, for one thing. It was security from heat, from noise, from trespassers. It was security from human danger, if you needed it for that. Once you learned how to survive in the jungle, you knew what to eat, what leaves to look at, what vines to cut if you didn't have water. There were water vines everywhere. You could just cut one. You weren't drinking; you were taking drips, but a lot of it. Once you learned that, you fell in love with the jungle, because it was security, plus it was so visual and visceral at the same time, because you come into the jungle and immediately there's a hush. And then you just stand there for a few minutes, and all the noises would come back. The frogs, the monkeys, whatever's trekking through there. You start seeing things. The butterflies start coming back out. The birds start flying again and pecking or whatever. But when you initially go in there, they're looking at you like, "Who the hell is that? Oh, that's Gene. It's okay. He isn't hunting. We can go back to what we were doing." So yeah, I'm really infatuated with the jungle, especially that triple canopy jungle, because it was a lifesaver, because the heat was unbearable at times. Going into that jungle and being able to sit down and not be bothered for a few moments. Because even though Jonestown was in the middle of the jungle, it itself was noisy. Either the pumps were going, or Mr. Muggs the chimpanzee was screaming, or people were screaming, and you've got a thousand people in just a few acres. It's just noise. The kitchen never shuts down. Even though it isn't serving you much, it never shuts down. They had a thousand people to feed, and people were on different schedules. There were shifts: day, swing, grave. The radio room was staticky all day long, every day. And you had Jones on the loudspeaker.

But it didn't affect me in a negative way, because I was there only a week or so and then I got yellow fever. Then Ollie had the baby. Then they put me in the shoe shop with Chuck Beikman, because I couldn't work in the field. Then, from the shoe shop, I went to the wood crew so I was away from the encampment. So I didn't go through that whole thirty days of indoctrination of like, "You gotta work thirty days in the field to become equal." I was willing to do it, but I didn't have to. And so, even in Jonestown, there were breaks for me. And that might have been the reason they said, "We need you to go to Georgetown to work with Guyanese customs." Because there were plenty of people that were more gifted, or as gifted, that could have gone to Georgetown to handle customs, and it wasn't like I was this great individual or anything. I was a stand-up person, and I understood business to a certain extent, because the construction crews in California still had to work even with Jack Beam being gone. So I understood organization, and I understood camaraderie and how to build crews. But that doesn't do it doing customs. It was just the opposite: With customs, you're dealing with an individual. And dealing with the different ministers and secretaries was kind of weird, because they're on a British type of political system. So there's lords and all that kind of stuff. That was definitely different. I had to learn that. But I actually enjoyed it, because it's like if you stay in your lane, you're okay. So it's cool. You have no reason to get out of your lane, because you know you're not a lord, you're a subject.

It was unheard of for somebody like me, being there such a short length of time, to be sent away from Jonestown. I look back, and anybody who would have stood up, that had stood up here in the States, had shown they would stand up, they were all in Georgetown with me. People who had argued or debated or said, "Oh no, we're not going for that." In Jonestown, there was no hierarchy, no independent governing bodies or authorities. It was just Jim Jones. His wife Marceline, in my opinion, had been emotionally assassinated already. Jones had his concubines, and those who wouldn't cooperate he just had drugged up: "Keep them down there in the cottage." Jones took an affinity to Shanda James Oliver, Ronnie James's younger sister and Bruce Oliver's wife, but when she made plain that she wasn't interested in him, all of a sudden she got ill. She didn't even know her own name. What kind of illness is that? It was a bad scene.

Jones was able to convince people to love the cause more than themselves. We all know that, in order to love somebody else, you must love yourself first. But in the case of Jones, he was able to convince some people to love the cause more than they loved themselves, and that was considered unselfish. But when you love something more than you love yourself, do you actually love yourself?

As I said, before I left San Francisco, Leona Collier, who was one of Jones's confidants, had said to me, "Eugene, when you get there, don't open your mouth. Don't say nothing. Just listen. I'm gonna be there in a couple months. If you're in danger or Ollie's in danger, you let me know, and I'll get you guys out." She was looking out for me, because I had become her driver, which had taken me off the construction crew. After I became Leona's personal driver, I'd had a few fights, and she said, "You and Ollie, you guys come and stay at my house, until she's ready to go. Then after she's gone, you stay here at the house, until you're ready to go." I said, "Okay." Then, when Leona arrived in Jonestown, the paranoia was so high that I couldn't even make eye contact with her, because they knew we were close. One thing about the Temple was that, if they knew you were close to somebody, that was your weakness and they used it against you. Either they went after them, or they went after you.

The level of paranoia was so high that I couldn't tell my own wife how I felt, or that I had plans to get us both out. I couldn't tell my best friend, Beau, who was there as well. But he was on the basketball team, so it was cool. I'd hung out with all the members of the basketball team at one time or another, but once we got there, friendships changed. At that point, I became an individual. There was no support system. Jack Beam had been my protector back in the States, almost from day one. But I couldn't go to him anymore, because in Jonestown, Jack didn't have power. I wanted to tell Ollie what I had in mind, but I couldn't. But then what happened was that they set up a concert, for our best singers and musicians to go to Georgetown to play for the prime minister, and the Jonestown basketball team would play the Guyanese international team. So I said, "Fantastic." Because Ollie would bring the baby with her.

And when I went to Georgetown in the first place Lee Ingram said, "Hey, Eugene, they want you to go to Georgetown."

I said, "It ain't gonna happen. I got a newborn baby. I'm happy. I'm having fun. Not interested."

A few days pass, maybe a week or so. "Hey, you know, really, Oliver has to come out of town. He's not making it in this customs stuff."

"What's that got to do with me?"

"Well, we think you'd be perfect for the position."

"I don't think so."

A few weeks pass, and Lee comes back to me: "Father wants you to go." That's like a threat. In other words, if you say no to this, your family is compromised. Ollie's not going to get that great care she's getting. She's not going to be able to stay in the nursery. She's not going to be able to walk around and not be harassed. She's not going to work in the fucking field with everybody else, but she's going to be working in the kitchen or something. Not that that's bad, but Ollie enjoyed working in the nursery. She had a newborn of her own, and it only made sense for him to be with the other new babies. And there was a hierarchy, and Ollie was not the low person, and neither was I. And I had to keep it that way, because I had no other way to escape. At least not until Martin was at least six months old; then I could take him into the bush. I wasn't yet well versed enough on jungle survival, to take a two- or three-month-old baby through that bush, or even just trekking down the road to Port Kaituma. The Venezuelan border wasn't that far away, but it might as well have been a million miles away.

So I said okay. "When is the basketball team going there? Tell them I'll be ready to go there in a few weeks. Ollie's gonna be singing. Here's my deal. She's coming into Georgetown, correct?"

"Yes. We promise you that she's definitely coming into Georgetown. We definitely want her to perform for the prime minister."

"Not a problem. The baby coming with her?"

"Of course the baby's coming with her."

"Okay." I wanted to be able to talk to her every day on the shortwave radio. "Okay. All right. We've got a deal. She's in town within a month or so, couple months. She's gonna sing for the prime minister. And I'll be returning. Correct?"

"Yeah."

"Okay."

And you know the rest now. Congressman Ryan and the Concerned Relatives arrived before the basketball team was able to play, and before Ollie was able to perform for the prime minister. And that just shortcut everything. And the paranoia was so high that I couldn't tell her. But since she was coming into Georgetown, I could easily take her on a tour of the city and slip into the US Embassy with her and Martin, and never show up again. That was the plan.

PART TWO

SURVIVING SURVIVAL

CHAPTER 6
Aftermath

After Jonestown, and after eight months with J. W. Osborne and his family in Compton, I moved back to Fresno and lived in the water tower in my mom's friend Mary Cromer's backyard. But after a while I had to get out of Fresno, because I was running across people I had grown up with, who knew where I had been and what I had done. Some were positive, but some were very negative. And Fresno's a much smaller place than LA or the Bay Area. And wherever I'm at, it's not that I tend to be noticed, but I end up doing something that's noticeable. It is what it is. People knew me from high school, and they knew that I had been an organizer, like in ninth grade when I organized the walkout on Martin Luther King's birthday and it wasn't even a holiday yet. I became vice president of the Black Student Union in the tenth grade because, although the president was popular, I felt I could manipulate him to get more things done. I had challenged the dean at Fresno High on different subjects. I had been on the wrestling team and made first string, and I snapped a guy's arm and laughed at him, because he tried to chicken wing me and I was much stronger than him. What I didn't understand was that when you're on the same team, you have to give people breaks. As far as I'm concerned we're on the same team, but if you're challenging me, you're challenging me.

So I left Fresno and moved back to the Bay Area, to Richmond in the East Bay, and I got in contact with family friends and extended family there, from my life prior to Peoples Temple. It was a way of connecting, but at the same time of keeping a certain distance.

I moved to Richmond because my best friend, Beau, gave me a call when I was in Fresno and working at the Aaron Brothers Art Mart there. Beau and I had reconnected through surreptitious channels, and there were no hard feelings between us about how he and my other friends, like Eddie Crenshaw and Joe Wilson, had shunned me when I first arrived in Jonestown, because I understood about the level of paranoia that had prevailed there. We had both survived and made it back to the world, so we found each other and resumed our friendship.

"You ready to come back to the Bay Area?" he asked me.

"Fuck yeah," I said.

"Well, we got a place, man. Come on up when you're ready."

"Okay. I'll see if I can get a transfer."

In Fresno I had been an assistant teacher and then worked at Aaron Brothers Art Mart as a matter/fitter. When Beau called me and offered me a place to stay in Richmond, I talked to my boss and he said, "Yeah, we're opening up an Aaron Brothers Art Mart in Richmond at Hilltop. You can transfer up there. I'm gonna be in Daly City, if you wanna come over there as well." His name was Don Gilbert. Really great guy. I said, "Okay, put in the transfer paperwork." So I transferred to the Aaron Brothers at Richmond Hilltop.

Over the couple years following November 18, 1978, there was a spate of killings and suicides of former Peoples Temple members. Different people being shot. I can't recall all the names, but many former members were getting injured or murdered. One of the first was actually before Jonestown, when Chris Lewis, whom I had become friends with, was assassinated on Fell Street in San Francisco. Chris was well known in the Fillmore. He operated there on the street level. At the same time, he was Jones's protector. I remember telling Chris one day, "Chris, man, I'm tired of this Temple shit. I want out." He said to me, "What do you want to do?" I said, "I want to hang with you, man. I want to be out here fighting the law." He said, "Just stay right here. You don't want to be out here where I'm at, because where I'm at will get you killed." I thought he was just thinking like, "I'm gonna protect this kid. He doesn't really know what's happening." Chris was assassinated on Fell Street, and to this day his murder hasn't been solved. He was one of Jones's personal guards on and off over the years. Everyone knew Chris in and around the Fillmore, and in San Francisco in general. I didn't get firsthand knowledge of the hit. It came out in the newspaper.

On March 13, 1979, when I was still living in Compton, Mike Prokes committed suicide. Mike was a former TV reporter from Modesto who had become the Temple's main spokesperson and press contact. On November 18, along with Tim and Mike Carter, Mike had left Jonestown through the jungle with instructions from Maria Katsaris to deliver a suitcase full of money to the Soviet Embassy in Georgetown. I was always cool with Mike. He was a good guy, as far as I knew. But he followed instructions. They never made it to the Soviet Embassy. They buried the suitcase near the chickery, before they even left Jonestown, because it was too heavy. But that's how Mike Prokes managed to survive the mass murder-suicide. But he didn't really survive, because on March 13 he called a press conference in a motel room in Modesto, read a statement to the eight reporters that showed up, then went in the bathroom and shot himself in the head. A note was found on him that read:

> Don't accept *anyone's* analysis or hypothesis that this was the result of despondency over Jonestown. I could live and cope with despondency.
>
> Nor was it an act of a "disturbed" or "programmed" mind – in case anyone tries to pass it off as that.
>
> The fact is that a person can rationally choose to die for reasons that are just, and that's just what I did.
>
> If my death doesn't prompt another look at what brought about the end of Jonestown, then life wasn't worth living anyway.

Another incident was when Al and Jeannie Mills, known during their Temple years as Elmer and Deanna Mertle, were murdered in their home in Berkeley on February 26, 1980. Jeannie and Al were early defectors from the Temple, and Jeannie was one of the cofounders of the Concerned Relatives. There were a few rumors of a Temple hit, but there were also stories of a drug deal gone bad. Their son, who was in the house at the time, was briefly suspected in the murders. But Al and Jeannie's murder, like the murder of Chris Lewis, remains unsolved. After a while the stories and rumors and incidents slowed down, from every week to every other week to every month, but for two or three years after Jonestown there was a strong vibe of menace and paranoia, and it was justified. I didn't see it at the time, but it was the same story as before still being told, on a smaller scale and back stateside.

All the killings and suicides and paranoia in the aftermath of Jonestown finally got to the point where Lynda Sykes, the second-oldest daughter and "junior mother" of the family that had embraced and fed and watched over me growing up in Fresno, said to me, "You need to get out of California for a while." She feared for my safety. She said, "I'm going to Oklahoma, and you're going with me." Lynda's mom had decided that I needed to get out of town, because they were reading in the papers about former Temple members committing suicide, getting shot, getting arrested. Mr. and Mrs. Sykes were reading this as, "You're in danger. We're gonna save you because we know you from a kid."

I hadn't known the Sykes family were in Richmond until I was already in Richmond myself and calling around to Fresno people and others. "Oh, you know Lynda's up in Richmond." "Oh really? Okay, cool." Lynda's daughter Roylynda was basically my god-niece. It was a good thing. I was able to see her again and connect with people who had known me before all the shit. They didn't really talk about Jonestown, which I appreciated. It was like, "Remember when we were kids, remember when we used to go rabbit hunting?" That kind of stuff. It was a comfortable environment. Lynda's husband Lonnie was in the National Guard. Weaponry. So that worked for me too, because I was going to the range on a regular basis at that time. Anyway, Lynda said, "Look, I need to go to Oklahoma anyway to check on the property. I'm gonna be down there for a while. You need to get out of here. I don't feel comfortable about it. Just get away for a while." I was like, "Okay, we can do that."

The Sykes family understood Black wealth. What I mean by that is that they understood that you must own property. You must have skill sets. You must know how to farm. They understood those things. They didn't drum it into my head, but they made me understand that it's something you must strive for. If you can't strive for that, at least learn the basics. Know how to farm. Know how to grow your own food. Know where your food comes from. Treat people the way you want to be treated. Mrs. Sykes was part of the Eastern Star, and Mr. Sykes was one of the highest-ranked Masons in California. They had both risen through the ranks. I didn't understand the importance of that at that time. I do now, and it has helped me in navigating through the rest of my life.

At that time I didn't really have a job, although I was still working at the Aaron Brothers Art Mart in Richmond. So we got in this '72 Dodge van and drove to Boley, Oklahoma. We lived there in a mobile home on some property the Sykes family owned on the main street at the edge of town. They had lots of property in downtown Boley, which is two blocks long. There were actually two mobile homes on the lot we stayed on. The other one was rented out, and the weird thing was that the people renting it claimed to have escaped from Jonestown. Lynda asked me if I knew them. I said no, because I didn't, and then the next morning they were gone. Weird.

I stayed in Boley for a few months and worked in construction, helping build the high school, which Lynda actually designed. My experience on the Peoples Temple construction crew stood me in good stead. Boley was founded in 1903, in the Creek Nation of what was then Indian Territory, about an hour and a half east of Oklahoma City. It was part of what became known as Black Wall Street, the famous all-Black towns of Oklahoma. The Boley Rodeo, founded in 1905, is a notable annual event, well known throughout the South. Booker T. Washington visited Boley often and championed it as "the largest and wealthiest Negro town in the world." In 1932, Pretty Boy Floyd declined to rob Boley's bank, saying, "There's no money there, and plus, those people have guns."

Boley's population was once as large as four thousand, but when I was there it had dwindled to about three hundred. The largest employer is the nearby prison, but the most important business is Smokaroma, a manufacturer of barbecue pits. The Boley phone book was twenty-three pages, with whole sections of a single family name: Sykes, Smith, Jones. All these multi-generational families, in a Black town. It was like, "Wow, this is kind of cool." Downtown was two blocks long, and the residential areas were about two blocks on each side. There was no jail. There was a holding cell with a bathroom, and that was it. There was a little restaurant right on the highway that cut through the town. Boley was good for me too because it brought me back to nature. I could go squirrel hunting after work and shoot my rifle off. People in Boley hunted, not for sport but for food. I ran into a lot of Black cowboys from the Boley Rodeo. It was interesting meeting Black cowboys. They were like, "This is my life. This is not a style statement. This is what I do." I also met Lynda's uncles, who were farmers and ranchers, and I learned how to haul hay and did some wildcat work on the oil fields. All in all, I got some life experience in Boley.

There were some rednecks just outside of Boley. I remember a particular incident where a redneck couple were trying to sell their car to somebody I was with, and they had a baby, and the husband popped the hood.

The wife set the kid on the ground, and the kid's running around, so she grabs the kid back up and she's holding it. The car won't start. In those days, cars still had carburetors. It wasn't fuel injected. So she's leaning under the hood too, with her boyfriend or husband and the guy I'm with. I'm standing back and looking at it. They pour some gas into the carburetor to prime it, and this flame comes up and everybody jumps back, and the baby's diaper catches on fire. And the wife is standing around stomping, running in a circle with the baby, and I'm saying, "Drop the baby. Drop the baby." So finally she drops the baby, and we put the baby out. She's running, and it's like, "I don't fucking believe this. Why would you even be leaning over a car engine with a baby in diapers anyway?" So obviously, the guy I was with didn't buy the car. There was a little bit of a discussion. Days later, we find out from the sheriff that they want to sue this guy for burning their baby. It was like, "No, she was leaning over the car too, plus it was their car." That was backwoods ignorance on a level that I wasn't quite ready for. I had seen *The Beverly Hillbillies* as a kid, but I didn't know they were real.

I stayed down there about three months, until there was snow on the ground, and then I came back. I caught the Greyhound bus home. Before I did, I went to the Woolworth's or something and bought a Marlin .22. I've got my little rifle bag and everything. What was funny was that in Oklahoma it was okay to travel with a weapon. But a law had passed that you couldn't travel on interstate buses with weapons. Well, I wasn't going to give up my rifle, so I wrapped it up in something. The bus was an express to California. I had to transfer in LA, so I had to claim the rifle. I'm watching them unload my rifle from the bus, and I see the guy looking at it and I'm thinking, "You fucking take that rifle, I'm gonna break your fucking neck." Then I go over to the counter and grab it from him. I said, "That's all right, I'm getting off here, going to LA." I didn't get off there. I actually got back on another bus. Made it to Richmond with my rifle and got off and went home. I think back on that now and I'm like, "You'd go to jail over a frickin' .22?" There are times in my life when I've done things that were really bad but I didn't have to pay for them. But I was always aware of that. I was lucky that time. I was lucky that I intimidated that guy enough to make him give the gun to me, but not enough to where he needed to tell somebody, "This guy's gonna hurt somebody."

So I picked up where I had left off in Richmond. Mrs. Sykes understood and encouraged me to go home. As far as she was concerned, the danger was over. It had been a few months; things had died down. They were no longer running news articles in the paper about Peoples Temple members committing suicide or being shot or being involved in something.

But the FBI fucked with me for years. They followed me and harassed me, starting with the interrogation at JFK Airport in New York. They had me listed in their file, identified by Odell Rhodes as part of the hit team. Anybody who was in the Temple knew that I didn't get along with any of the Jones boys. Not Lew, not Tim, not Jimmy, not Stephan, not even the extended family. Odell could have said any name but mine. But he didn't. He said my name, Eugene Smith, and as a result the FBI hounded my ass. I want the reader, you, to know that just because you didn't do anything, doesn't mean you're not being watched. I want you to feel the anxiety that I felt in those early years of my life after Jonestown. I need for your heart to skip a beat, or to race for a few seconds. I want you to say to yourself, "I never saw it like that." Because, believe me, nothing about America has really changed in the forty-plus years since then.

CHAPTER 7
Too Busy to Grieve

After returning from Oklahoma I applied for the East Bay Skills Center to learn industrial maintenance, which is working on things like motors, engines, generators, HVAC, aircon, heating. Standard Oil was hiring, and a teacher named Roger Simmons told me, "Eugene, you should really take this test." Standard Oil noticed me there and picked me up because I had a mechanical background, and I also had very good perception. I didn't know that I was applying for multiple jobs in the processing of crude oil, and that your score dictated the type of plant you would work in. Basically, the less computerized the more physical, and vice versa. They gave you tests on perception: You had a square, and the square was 144 squares, and they take a section of it out: How many squares are there now? In your mind you had to see all the squares, and I could do that. It was easy for me. So out of five hundred people being considered for a particular job at Standard Oil, they hired sixty of us. And I was one of the sixty, and out of the sixty I was in the top ten percent. That got me in a mechanized plant producing jet fuel and railroad diesel, operating equipment remotely via computer. I operated the mid-distillate hydrofiner, checking every shift for pressure, level, flow, temperature. So that meant I didn't have to go out there and deal with bottoms and sludge and wax and stuff.

I had made a conscious decision that I needed to get a government job, whether federal, state, county, or city. Those were the only jobs I would consider, because I had to have a pension. I had to have retirement, because I hadn't learned to save money. I had to have a job that did that for me, that took the money and set it aside before it got to me. It wasn't that I particularly liked governments. But I had to have a pension, and that was how I planned to get one. But I had to take a long route to get there, because I had to create a work record. I even applied to be a glow boy. A glow boy is someone who inspects the wall thicknesses on nuclear reactors. I applied for that, but Standard Oil hired me first. Standard Oil was my first real job.

And then, just six months to the day after I started, I had my motorcycle accident. After six months working at Standard Oil, I was finally going to get weekends off. You only got weekends off three months out of every year. The rest of the time you worked a rotating shift, going from day to grave to swing, which is the hardest. Usually you try to transition day, swing, grave, but they believed in day, grave, swing, because that was what worked for them. Most of the guys at Standard Oil were ex-military, and I was able to fit in with them because I had the same type of mindset. I bought me a '76 Alfa Romeo Alfetta, and then a guy who worked for Standard Oil was being assigned to Saudi Arabia, and he had a 1988 Yamaha XS 1100. At that time that was the biggest bike out there, so I bought it.

And I drove up to the front gate, took my helmet off, put on my racing goggles, and said, "I'm not gonna take the highway home. I'm gonna go the slow road. I'ma go through Point Richmond." So I turned out the gate, and I went up Tewksbury Avenue. This was off the beaten path. I didn't want to go down Hoffman Boulevard or Cutting Boulevard. I wanted to take the slow road home. I was really going to enjoy this. I was going to stop by the beach.

And just as I reached the crest of the hill, a '53 Dodge pickup made a left turn. I impacted the passenger side bumper. I was in a coma for thirteen days. As I was coming out of the coma, I started hearing again. All the machines in my hospital room were going, because I was on life support. I woke up and everything was kind of blurred, and I knew something was wrong; I just couldn't say what it was. So I pulled out the catheter, pulled the stuff out of my throat—they had had to cut a trach because I had quit breathing. That's what got me into a coma; I had lost oxygen. And I'm looking around like, "Where the fuck am I?" I didn't know, because I had gone into a coma within hours of being picked up off the road. I hit the buzzer, because I couldn't open or close my hand. It was just stuck in a grip. The nurse came in and said, "Oh, my God!" So before she called the doctor they put everything back in, but there was no anesthesia this time. So then they call the doctor, who comes up and says, "Take it all out." So they take it all out. And then my extended family came in, including Lynda Sykes. I could feel that my teeth were messed up.

I said, "Show me a mirror." They refused. "Show me a mirror. I'm asking you. Please show me a mirror." So Lynda showed me a mirror, and I cried, and I told her, "What have I done to my face?" It was just shattered. My teeth were shattered. My nose was broken and swollen. My eyes were off center. I had bruised my cheeks. I couldn't open or close my hand. My legs were swollen. But I didn't know that I had done all the cartilage damage, because they didn't have MRIs in those days.

So they say, "Can you stand up?"

"Sure," I said. And I stood up and fell right over.

"Oh, you might wanna stay in here a couple days."

"No. I wanna go home." So I called my best friend Beau: "Hey, man. Come get me."

"We want you to stay a couple days," the doctor said.

"I don't wanna stay. I don't wanna stay."

"Okay. We'll release you." So they released me.

And I had been on a liquid diet, because I'd been in a coma, obviously. So to Beau I said, "Stop by Nation's Burgers. I want a slice of cheesecake, a milkshake, and a burger." I ate that. I got home, and there were a few friends visiting. "Hey Gene, wanna party?" "Sure." I took a toke, and I snorted some cocaine. I went into my room, and I didn't come out for three days. I couldn't come down. I said, "Oh, I'll never do nothing like that again." And so that was it for drugs. They're like, "Oh, man, come on. You wanna party?" And I was like, "No, I don't."

Then I realized that I couldn't walk. So I went back in, and they put ink in there, and they could see where I had torn my meniscus and severed my ligaments. My leg could bend in a weird way, because there was nothing there. I had surgery to rebuild my knee every three months for a year. And I was off work that first year, then a second year. I had Long Term Disability insurance with Standard Oil, because guys got injured all the time. I had applied for that when I first got hired on. And I had made my probation, so I was able to access that insurance for a couple years. Then I went back to work, and I was at the refinery and I was climbing over one of the stills, and I felt my leg release. I was like, "Oh. Oh, it feels great. Fantastic." But then within days, my leg started swelling up and this yellow gunk was coming out of my knee where the incisions had been, and I go in, and my leg was infected, and it turned out that they had left the suture material in. So they went back in and removed that, and I was off work again. So I pulled my motorcycle out of the garage, started it up, and said, "Okay, I'm gonna take it for a ride."

I didn't give up motorcycles, because I needed the adrenaline rush. So on my 1100, which had been completely restored thanks to insurance, I'm driving up Fruitvale Avenue. I go into the Diamond District, the Diamond Meat Market. I do my shopping. My saddlebags are full. Now I'm coming back down Fruitvale, and the light turns yellow, so I drop it from third to second. I wind it up. I'm gonna run this light. Nah. Nah, Eugene. What are you doing, man? What's wrong with you? So I stop at the light, and I'm rocking my bike from side to side with my feet on the ground. I put it in first gear and I'm feeling good, looking up like, "Wow, this feels so good, to be on my bike again."

And then the next thing was that I had only the sensation of being. I knew that I was present, but I couldn't feel anything. I'm looking around, and all I can see is blue. According to the guys across the street I was twenty feet in the air, and I had gone into a backwards somersault, which is why all I could see was blue. Someone hit me at roughly thirty-five miles an hour, never hit their brakes, didn't realize there was a stop light there. I look over my left shoulder and I can see my motorcycle. It's in front of a car. I come down on the hood of that car in a fetal position: Bam! And it bounces me back up. But this time I had my helmet on. I'm sitting on the car with my legs in front of me but not dangling, and I'm holding onto the hood. The car continues across the intersection, then crosses the center divide, hits another car head on, with me on the hood. I slide off, take my helmet off. I had on a black Arai racing helmet. All this side is white where I've impacted. I walk across the street and look back at my bike. It was a shaft drive. The shaft is demolished and my rear tire, rear rim, which was some kind of synthetic material, had shattered, and the seat is pointing straight up. When he hit me, I had gone into a backwards somersault, and the guys across the street said, "I don't believe it, man. You were fucking in the air, dude. You won't believe it." Screaming and shit. The paramedics show up and say, "Where's he at?" Because the bike is demolished. I say, "I'm right here." They say, "What? Hold on. We gotta check you out." So they check me out. They say, "Wow. You're okay." I had a headache. You know I had a headache. But I walked away from it.

I never got on bikes again after that. The man that hit me was eighty-five years old, hadn't had a wreck in thirty or forty years, and he said normally the insurance company would've dropped him already, but he just slipped through.

So I had to quit working for Standard Oil because, first of all, I had trouble climbing. I had to be able to climb the stills because I made jet and diesel fuel, which meant that, even though it was a highly mechanized plant that was run by computer, I still had to check levels physically. Jet fuel flashed at room temperature, and I made railroad diesel for Alaska that wouldn't gel in the cold up there. When the fuel gels and you're in a train, that's really bad news because you can't do anything, you just sit there and freeze. So anyway, I didn't go back to Standard Oil. I started applying for jobs again, and I went to the Private Industry Council in Oakland. The Private Industry Council basically said if you're a business coming to Oakland, you will hire Oakland people first. And I got in with that, learned how to take interviews and how to do my resumes. And I moved from Richmond to Oakland.

I ended up being a building inspector in Oakland for maybe two years. And I still hadn't grieved yet. I was still trying to find a job that I could hold onto, and now that I was injured, it was like I didn't need this—grieving for my mother, wife, and child, and for what had happened at Jonestown—in my life right now. I called C.E. Engineering and they said, "Well, we're not hiring right now." I had lab skills because I had worked in a laboratory at Standard Oil, doing testing on fuels and reactor waters. So I kept calling C.E. Engineering and the guy says, "Look man, what's your name again? Eugene? Look, come on down, take your interview, but I'm not hiring. I'm just tired of you calling."

So I go down there and he says, "You mind getting dirty?" I say, "You gonna pay me to get dirty?" He says, "Yeah, I'll pay you. Tell you what. I'll hire you for one day. If you like the job, it's yours. If you don't, I'll pay you for one day." I was there for three years, then from there I went to doing special inspections. I was doing concrete inspections on work sites. Every hundred yards I had to take four samples in plastic cylinders twelve inches high and six inches across, which would be tested for compressive strength, pounds per square inch, at seven, fourteen, and twenty-one days. The fourth cylinder would be kept for years in a humidified environment, just in case there was a failure. I was doing rebar inspection for sidewalks and walls. C.E. Engineering was a testing lab, usually contracted either by the city or by the contractor on the yard to hand in to the city. In other words we're doing everything per UBC, Uniform Building Code.

Prior to the first time I went out as a concrete inspector the guy told me, "They're gonna treat you different, Eugene, because you're Black." Again. And they did. But it wasn't so much that I bore it, I made them bear me. When you go over to Emeryville and you see all the new apartments over there, I was one of many concrete and rebar inspectors for that. When you go to Livermore, look at all the buildings on the left-hand side going from the Dublin Grid to the Altamont Pass. I was one of many inspectors on all those buildings. The buildings in Livermore are tilt-ups, meaning that the walls are poured concrete that's placed while the wall is flat on the ground, and after thirty days the wall is tilted up and attached. That was when the boom was coming on in the Bay Area, in the late 1980s. So I did that and then I pretty much burned out, and then I got hired on at Bank of America, transferring currency to the foreign currency exchange at the San Francisco Airport. Totally different job, like a Brinks truck driver. I would have duffle bags of foreign currency, and I'd be dragging it down the terminal, nobody knew it was maybe a quarter of a million dollars, and then on Sunday mornings I would leave San Francisco and meet the drivers coming from LA in Kettleman City, and we'd have a bill of lading. I'd give them my bill of lading, they'd give me their bill of lading, I'd give them my van keys, they'd give me their van keys. We'd transfer. All my stuff goes to LA, their stuff goes up to San Francisco. And then from that I ended up being at Japan Airlines as the forklift driver unloading the airplanes coming in, and that was cool because I understood customs from doing it for Peoples Temple in Guyana. So that worked out for me.

And then I got serious. I said, "Okay, I gotta find a government job." City, county, federal, or state. And Caltrans, the California Department of Transportation, was just a block away on Van Ness. At this point I was thirty-three or thirty-four. My thing was, I'm gonna give them twenty years, I want to retire at fifty-five. I'm not gonna work till I'm sixty years old. I refused to do that, because I worked my fucking ass off as a kid and as a teenager at Peoples Temple. I'll be damned if I'm gonna work all the way into old age. So I applied with Caltrans, and from the day I went in and filled out the application to the day I walked in the door to start work there was almost two years. After I started, the regional manager, Chet Moran, summoned me to his office in Walnut Creek. After we sat down he said to me, "You must be smart?" I'm thinking, "Is that a question or a comment?" That's when he told me that, during the interview process, he had instructed his maintenance managers that he wanted a Black person, and he wanted that person to be smart.

That was September 1992, when I actually hired on with Caltrans. And I worked at Caltrans until January 31, 2015, age fifty-seven. I did two years more than I intended to, because we had a recession. The recession set me back a couple of years.

Through all of this, I still hadn't grieved. I didn't have time to grieve. I was too busy trying to become a success, and trying to get my adrenaline under control. I used to drive from Oakland to Fresno in an hour and forty-five minutes. That's a two-and-a-half-hour drive. I'd top out at 140. But that made me happy. Some of it was like the behavior of a military veteran, which is why working with the military guys at Standard Oil was perfect, because we had the same mindset. We all had our PTSD we were dealing with. It was just that some had been diagnosed and some hadn't. At that time they called it battle fatigue. Or war syndrome. There was no PTSD. "It's not me, I just like to go fast." But that's what it was. Which is why I bought an Alfa Romeo. I like to go fast. I like being scared. Just on the edge, and then going past that.

I used to go to Mexico just about every year, all through the eighties and nineties. I used to do the fifty-mile fun ride from Rosarito to Ensenada. It's a fifty-mile ride on a mountain bike and you do it on the Libre Road, which is unmaintained. There's no guardrails. On one part of that road is a hill called El Tigre. It's a 7.5 percent grade over a couple of miles. It's hell. Then you reach the mesa for three miles, and then you go downhill for three or so miles to sea level. It's super steep, with lots of curves and no guardrails. At fifty miles per hour on a mountain bike it's incredible, and worth the effort. There's nothing like it. When you ride the course backwards and you look over the edge, you look down and see all these rusted cars where there was a guardrail but they went through it, and some new cars down there too that haven't rusted yet. They give you five hours to complete the fifty-mile course. If you don't, they open the road back up, and now you're competing on a one-lane road going around the side of a mountain with no guardrail. The first time I got introduced to it, I had a Mexican girlfriend at the time. She said, "Let's go to Mexico for vacation, and we'll do it on a poor man's diet." So we caught the plane to LA, caught the bus to the border, walked across the border. Stayed in Tijuana a couple days and went over to a guy: "Hey, we'd like to catch the bus to Rosarito." He looked at us and said, "We don't got no places for you." So I'm like, "What the . . . ?" I'm going off, and Julia said, "Gene, you're not in America. We can catch the next bus." And I turned into the ugly American. "Fuck that!" I'm fucking American. That's not right, you know? But we caught the next bus.

And so we're on the bus. People had chickens. They had babies. They had fresh fruit, fresh vegetables. They had groceries, sundries, everything. Babies are crying and it's like, "This is kind of cool." Until the first checkpoint, where the guy asked specifically, "Are there any Americans on the bus?" I put my head in Julia's lap and just stayed there. Nobody said a word. All the people on the bus were Mexicans, Salvadorans, Guatemalans, Nicaraguans. Every Latino group you could think of was represented on that bus. It was the United Nations for Latin America. He came onto the bus. He walked down maybe two rows. "Any *americanos*?" He got back off, and that was it. What I realized was, that checkpoint was because there's the Libre Road and then you have the road that you pay a toll every few miles. That toll road, if you have an accident and you have Mexican insurance, which you should when you cross the border, you're cashed out. The Libre Road is for the locals and smugglers and for this particular bike race. I didn't know about the bike race then. I'm just on this bus. Any American on that bus on the free road, "What the fuck you doing?"

So we're going down this free road, and when I look out the window, I'm looking down and I'm not seeing road. We're going around these curves, and I put my head back in Julia's lap again, because when he would turn, the front end would swing off the road. I said, "I'm never doing this again." And then five or six years later, I'm going down that same road, fifty miles an hour on a mountain bike. But it's strange how things come back around to you, but they're presented in a different way. Makes me feel good. It's my drug. I'm not buying it, you know? There's no purchase with this. It's my adrenaline. It makes me feel good. It alerts me. I gain confidence from it. I gain security. Not everybody's willing to do it. Not everybody can. It's not about bravery. It's about challenges and meeting them. I always want to face any challenge as soon as I can, so it's behind me. Constantly facing something puts me on edge and makes me real agitated. But I force myself to face it immediately, so I can get it behind me as soon as possible, so it's at my back rather than at my front.

Six months after getting out of the hospital I did cocaine again, and it scared me. "No no no, I don't like this." I ended up passing out, and I didn't feel my pain. But the next morning when I woke up, I was in more pain than ever. I don't need anything that dulls the pain. I need to feel the pain, so I know it's there. So I never was into pain medications. After the accident, I just had to rough it out. To me pain is a signal, and you need to be aware of it, because when you're not aware of it, you end up doing more damage than you would have done. That was the last time I ever did cocaine.

I tried to get counseling when I first got back and was in LA, but they wanted me to make admissions that I wasn't willing to make. They said, "Are you willing to admit that you were programmed? Are you willing to admit that you were brainwashed?" I said, "Well, a person that's programmed or brainwashed doesn't know they need help. I'm asking for help." And they said, "Unless you admit this, there's nothing we can do for you." It was because people and agencies in the government were scared of us, and they needed something to validate the treatment we were getting.

I was done with them after that. That was in LA in '79. They were offering therapy to survivors, but you had to make all these admissions, and I wasn't willing to do that. I think their mentality was, "We can help these people, but they're gonna have to make some admissions, because this can't be normal. There can't be any normal people there. There has to be something wrong with all of them. Those few that survived, okay, they survived out of luck or whatnot. But something's wrong with them too, there has to be. And we're not gonna allow any funding to help them with mental issues, unless they're willing to admit this." Now that's an opinion, because I don't actually know what they were thinking. I just know that they asked me if I was willing to admit that I had been programmed. And I was like, "No, I'm not." To admit that would have been to go down a rabbit hole, and I think it would have come back to haunt me.

It even got to the point where they were offering settlements after they started selling off Peoples Temple entities and stuff, but you had to make admissions, and you got so many thousands of dollars for each life lost in your family. I wouldn't accept that. I called it, even then, and I still call it, blood money. I shouldn't have to fucking justify my child being dead or my wife being dead or my mother being dead, and I gotta admit something that's a lie to me. That's blood money. I'll do without. And I'm not gonna make an admission if I don't believe it. Period. And I always felt that if I did, it would come back to haunt me somehow. Even though they labeled us crazy anyway, it's like, "Well, you ain't got it on paper that I said it." And when I came back, as far as I was concerned, I was in enemy territory. And it wasn't about making it, it was about surviving it. Coming back here to the US was about surviving survival. I didn't explain things. I never even spoke to Ollie's family. They never really wanted to speak to me. And for twenty-seven years I said nothing.

Caltrans assigned me first to Orinda, California. I had signed up for highway maintenance. The same test also covered landscape maintenance, but I had allergies. But the guy said, "Look, just get hired on, go through your probation, which is six months, and then you can transfer." So I hired on with a crew in Orinda. I was the first Black guy on the crew. I'm always the first Black, wherever I go, and I was working there and I didn't know these people. So at lunchtime I'd always bring my lunch and I'd bring me something to read, and they'd be out doing whatever they're doing.

And they told the supervisor, "We don't trust him." And the supervisor asked them why, and they gave him some excuse. So he contacted the regional manager, Chet Moran. So Chet comes down and says, "Okay, Eugene, look, I just want you to be quiet and just listen." And then he said, "What's happening here?"

"Well, we don't trust Eugene."

"Does he do his job?"

"Yes."

"Does he follow instructions?"

"Yes."

"In addition to following instructions, does he do what he's told the way you describe it?"

"Yes, he does."

"Does he communicate with you?"

"Yes, he does."

"So what's the problem?"

"Well, we don't know what he's thinking." They were comfortable enough to say that. This is 1992.

And he says, "What does that have to do?"

"Well, when we have lunch, he's always reading."

And so Chet said, "Gene, go clean out your locker."

"What?"

"Go clean out your locker." So I go clean out my locker. He says, "Put all your stuff in my car." I put all my stuff in his car, and I'm sizzling, because I'm still maybe a month away from making my six months where I'd be a permanent employee, and this crops up.

But then Chet says, "So, you don't know what he's thinking? Okay, Eugene. You're now promoted. You're gonna be on the MPRO crew. You're gonna supervise the maintenance probationers. That's all we got to talk about today." Maintenance probationers were civilians who had traffic infractions, misdemeanors, DUIs and so on, and the court had ordered them to perform community work in lieu of jailing them. They picked up trash along the freeway, hoed weeds, and cleaned rest stops and maintenance yards.

And that was my stepping stone to state employment. But it was interesting: "We don't trust him."

"Why?"

"Because we don't know what he's thinking."

I don't know what I was projecting that gave them this fear, other than that I was still angry. Jonestown happened in '78, and in '92 I was still angry. My mental state was that I was angry, and that it was none of their business. Women and men go to war, and they don't talk about their experiences. They come back and that's the end of it, and they hold it in for the rest of their lives. And that's what I did. But the Jonestown anniversary would come around every year on November 18, and people would make these "Don't drink the Kool-Aid" jokes. And those jokes infuriate me. They make me want to take a baseball bat, and put spikes through it, and beat you with it.

There's a video clip that shows up in a lot of documentaries, that shows Jim Jones giving a tour of the Jonestown food stocks and pointing out a box of Kool-Aid packets. We did have some Kool-Aid, but in the amount that we're buying these drinks, we couldn't afford Kool-Aid. I remember Kool-Aid being like ten cents, and Flavor Aid was like five cents or seven cents, and when you're buying that in tens of thousands, that's money. Children, even if they're in Guyana in the jungle, have to have some normalcy some kind of way. There was no way to refrigerate the amount of sodas or Coca-Colas or Pepsis that would be necessary, not so much to make the kids happy, but just to give them a moment of joy. Children, even if you put them in an adverse environment, if you can occasionally give them some normalcy, they'll accept that environment. So we bought Flavor Aid, which was basically welfare Kool-Aid. When people say "Drink the Kool-Aid," it infuriates me, because we couldn't even actually afford Kool-Aid.

We knew we were going to get fruit drink or whatever, and Kool-Aid was on every commercial there was. The Kool-Aid kid, the picture with the smiley face of Kool-Aid. You never saw Flavor Aid commercials, because they didn't have any commercials. It was welfare. Now it's a catchphrase, like, "You're an idiot, you're stupid, you're programmed. You can't think for yourself." When I hear people say "Drink the Kool-Aid," it's almost like "Drink ignorance." It infuriates me. It angers me. It disgusts me. It's a low moment in the thought process of Americans. It makes me despise the person who said it. Recently I was watching *The View.* Usually the first fifteen minutes is political, and it gives me a little dose of news. I forget the lady's name; she had just had a baby. She said, "Well, you don't want to drink the Kool-Aid." She said it two days in a row. So I'm pretty much done with that show now, because people don't understand the hurt behind that. Let's just say that it was Kool-Aid, and they drank it. What gives you the fucking right to make light of that? They didn't do it because they wanted to. They were forced, they were coerced, and they were tricked.

People say it with bravado, like, "I know this." No, you don't. You listened to some media like forty years ago that said, "Oh, there was a big vat of Kool-Aid." That was the only thing they could associate it with, at the time. I don't blame them, but I do blame the people after that who just didn't read. They didn't research. They didn't look. They were like, "Fuck it. I accept that that's how it is. I didn't like them anyway, so that makes sense." It bothered me. Yeah, "They drank the Kool-Aid." It's a catchphrase. It's in the lexicon of American language. It's going to be here for decades to come. It should be, for Americans, "Don't drink the bullshit." I know you wonder about this, because I always say "the Americans," as if like, "Well, what the fuck are you?" Well, I'm an American that's left the country and looked back at it multiple times in my life, from multiple countries and multiple continents, and it ain't the beautiful thing we think it is.

Americans have the capacity to be vicious with a laugh behind it. I've never been able to grasp that, how they can laugh at death and then be appalled when somebody else does the same thing they did. That's where that "Drink the Kool-Aid" issue takes me. Even before I came out and told people that I was part of Peoples Temple, I always defended them about drinking Kool-Aid. I would be like, "You know, you really don't understand that."

And they'd say, "What do you know about it?"

"Oh, nothing, just stuff I read," and I'd move on. I wouldn't debate it or carry the conversation on.

"Well, how do you know?"

"I just know."

But they couldn't afford it. And since I was the one in customs in Georgetown with the people purchasing it, I knew it for a fucking fact. There might have been some Kool-Aid packages, but in terms of the gross amount, it was Flavor Aid.

CHAPTER 8
Learning Processes

I knew when I came back from Guyana that I'd never get married again, and that I'd never have children. Over the years I've run across people who have told me, "You should have kids, you could be a great dad." I've told them all, "I don't think so." I've had girlfriends who had children who told me, "You're better than their dad." But that's because the responsibility for their survival was not on me. So I can be good, with less pressure. When I got back I had a few relationships in LA, and they were fleeting. My sister-in-law in Compton, Bernadette, who was from Georgetown, had a friend named Pam, who was also Guyanese. Pam and I had this little fling or whatever. It was cool. But I didn't have any real relationship until probably '82, when I was working at Aaron Brothers Art Mart in Richmond, and I met a young lady. She entered an art contest, she had on these striped coveralls, had her hair in a big bun in the back, and she did this abstract that I thought was really cool.

And I said, "Is this what you do?"

"Oh, well you know, I want to be an artist." She was like eighteen, but she had started college at sixteen.

We started talking because she lived at Hilltop, and we started going out. So I told her, "I got something I gotta tell you. And I'm not gonna hold it against you, I respect you. If you want to have a relationship we can. But if you don't, I totally get it. This is my life, this is what happened to me, this is where I'm at."

She said, "Okay, cool. Wanna go to Golden Gate Park?" So we go to Golden Gate Park. Then she says, "Okay, I'm gonna introduce you to my mother." What I didn't realize was that her mother was white and her dad was Black. Her mother helped develop the polio vaccine, and her father worked on the first nuclear sub. Her mom immediately just embraced me. Not physically, but she embraced me emotionally, and she said, "It's okay." She was real comforting. This white mom is accepting me. Her daughter is like, "He's okay," and her mom is saying, "Yeah, he's okay, he's a good guy." Her dad, on the other hand, basically didn't like Black men, not for his daughter. But he didn't live with her. Our relationship lasted like ten years, and during it her parents got divorced and he moved on to another family.

What Catherine did for me was, she taught me how to read. Just like my mother taught me how to read, but in a different way. Catherine taught me *how* to read. When I came back, I had said, "I'm only gonna read stuff from Black authors, period. I'm not gonna read anything from white people." But Catherine read voraciously. She could sit down and read a novel over a weekend. Two hundred fifty pages over a weekend, she'd sit down and just do it. And then tell you about it. And then she'd do her art work. And she says, "Eugene?"

"Yeah babe, what's up?"

"What are you reading? Who's it by?"

"Oh, it's by this Black author."

"Do you read anything but Black authors?"

"No, I don't."

"Well, you're cheating yourself."

"What do you mean?"

"Because you have to have more than one viewpoint to have a judgment on it. You can't come up with a rational reason if you only read one side of the story. You have to read it from every aspect that you can, to have a rational conversation about it. You're really smart, but you're one-dimensional, because you're only reading one dimension."

I said, "Really? Okay." So then I started reading everything. And I was a better person for that because it allowed me to see things from as many angles, as many perspectives, as I possibly could. I might not want to do it, but if I have an interest in it, I'm going to read everything about it. I don't care who wrote about it.

"Look, take what you need, throw out the rest."

"Well, I don't like this because he said—"

"Forget what he said. There's another two hundred pages of him saying something else. Take what you need and leave the rest."

I got it. And that's how it was. Catherine was also the girlfriend I was with when I had the motorcycle accident, so I was off work for three years, I was crippled, and she helped me. I wasn't living with her at the time. We ended up moving in together later on, but by that time I was already doing building inspection at C.E. Engineering. So it was cool, but she became so valuable to me that I became overly protective. It's a mean world. I had lost Ollie, and I didn't want to lose Catherine too. I was not willing to accept any more losses.

Catherine introduced me to her friends, the majority of whom were white because she was raised in that environment. Her language skills dictated that. In other words, she was an excellent communicator, and she communicated to her friends that I wasn't dangerous. I was cool with all of them. And I was comfortable enough that I loaned her my Alfa Romeo to drive to LA with her friends, so they could go somewhere to see a concert. I had to love that woman to loan her my Alfa Romeo.

I didn't feel I had been stunted by Peoples Temple. I don't think I was stunted at all. I think I made an emotional choice to be ultra Black. But in order to be a Black man, you must know white people. You must read what they write, and you must read it vociferously and understand it and relate to it. Even if it has to be translated, figure it out if it's something that's important to what you're interested in. Not hate it, not like it, not despise it, just understand it and make it part of who you are, because you're in an environment where your oppressor understands you more than you ever understood him, because they've had over four hundred years to study us as slaves, as freedmen, during Jim Crow. These were all experiments that were taken on because they're afraid of us: of what we might do, or of our DNA. Whatever it might be, they put all these roadblocks in. If I don't understand that, I can't defend myself.

Slaves weren't allowed to read, unless it was the Bible. The Bible, as I see it, is almost like propaganda, because it's contradictory in its language. If you're a slave, you have a good master, be happy. The fuck am I gonna be happy? I'm a slave. Okay, I got a good master, so why am I happy about that? It's just contradictory. I look at the Bible as propaganda, and I look at missionaries as mercenaries. They use that weapon, and it was used against us, and it worked, and it's working. It doesn't mean that I don't read the Bible. What it means is that I look at as many different versions of the Bible as I can possibly afford, just to see what the differences are. I even had this Bible that came out in the 1800s. It was called the Slave Bible, and the passages in it were specifically geared towards creating a slave society and keeping it that way. So I understand that, and Catherine helped me understand that. So I'm forever grateful to her for that, because it opened me up to another world. If it had not been for her, it might've happened, but it might've happened so late that it wouldn't have been of any value to me. I would've been an agnostic or an atheist that was just fucking mad, but not really understanding why: "I just don't believe in that shit."

"What shit?"

"Well, you know, that shit, that bullshit."

"What bullshit?"

"You know."

That's the reason I don't relate to any of my relatives now, because even though they might've been thugs, thieves, players, and pimps, their fathers were ministers and deacons, and they're now their fathers and grandfathers. Because pimps and preachers are pretty much the same. One's pimping individuals, one's pimping a group. There's not a whole lot of difference there.

So Catherine taught me how to read. Catherine taught me how to really appreciate art for art's sake. Don't get into the artist, get into the work and what it means to you, how it affects you. When we broke up, it was on good terms. But we broke up because she outgrew me. I grew up, and she outgrew me. But we both knew that, so we were able to communicate on that level. She was younger than me, but she's the one that said, "What do you mean you only read Black authors? How can you possibly have a conversation and you only have one dimension of it?" So I grew up. I learned how to read again. She outgrew me, because she continued on. She was a painter, but she also did lithographs, pen and inks. She was multifaceted. She lives in Seattle now. I still stay in touch with her on and off. Every couple of years, one of us will call the other. I was very fortunate to find her. I lucked out, finding her.

And then there were a couple of relationships in between there that lasted a few years and whatnot. Not good, not bad, but I never had these knock-down, drag-out relationships where it was like, "I hate you." None of that. That's just not me. We don't have to leave being friends, we just have to leave each other respectfully. That's one of the things I'm pretty stable with. I'm not dysfunctional in that sense. There's a lot of dysfunction, that just isn't it.

So I get into my thirties and get involved with a woman who's fifty, named Julia. I was with Julia through most of my thirties. And, again, I'm in a learning process. And the learning process this time is, "Look, you might not always get the job you want, but you better damn sure work until you get there."

And I'm like, "That's not what I want. I don't want to do that."

"Well, fine, you don't want to do that. So you do it not wanting to do it, but you do it until you can do something else."

Julia's teaching me this. And it's like, "At the same time, Eugene, understand that this society is gonna judge you. Even if they don't know about Jonestown, even if they don't know about Peoples Temple, even if they don't know you lost your whole family. You're so fucking outspoken, you're gonna be looked at. You're gonna be observed, and you're gonna be judged. Are you ready for that? Now, if you're ready for that, continue to be outspoken, continue to be who you are. If you're not ready for that, tone it down and live with it." And I'm like, "Fuck that, I'm not toning down shit."

Julia and I split up in 1990 or '91. One point of contention near the end was that she wanted me to become a process server, because she saw that as stable employment. But no way was I going to knock on people's doors and serve subpoenas for a living. In any case, we parted ways amicably and I moved on.

It was September 1992 that I started at Caltrans. My priority was to get through probation and then do ten years to get fully tenured to secure a pension, and then everything after that would be icing on the cake. That meant that my focus was on keeping my head down, and my mantra became: "Let me just make it to 2002." Throughout that decade, I used my vacation time to go to Baja California twice a year. I enjoyed taking part every September in the fifty-mile Fun Ride from Rosarito to Ensenada. What I especially liked about Rosarito was that it was where the famous disc jockey Wolfman Jack used to be based. Julia and I had gone there to visit the location he had broadcast from.

Beau and I started talking about traveling together further afield. By 1998, it had been twenty years since the Jonestown incident, and our assumption was that the feds no longer considered us a threat to society, so we started making plans to go somewhere in 1999. At that time, Americans didn't need a passport to go to Mexico; all you needed was Mexican insurance and a driver's license. But to go anywhere else you needed a passport, so I applied for one. The State Department told me sure, I could have a passport, but first I had to pay them back three hundred and some dollars for flying me from JFK to LA on New Year's Eve 1978, after the incident. I remember thinking, "Shit, back then three hundred and some dollars should have bought me a seat in First Class." It irked me to have to pay the feds back for that flight, but I did, and I got my passport.

From time to time I considered moving out of the US entirely. I considered moving to Mexico, until they shot the mayor of Tijuana. There were 110 bullet holes in the trunk of his car, and most of those were in him. I considered Costa Rica, but Costa Rica is now a way point for the dealers bringing cocaine into the US. It's not safe there for expats. I considered mainland Mexico, but the way politics go there you could be five miles out of Mexico City and you might as well be on an island, and you can be arrested and never heard from again. Whereas in Baja, you're still affected by Mexico's rule, but because you're just two hours from the border, you have an escape.

But in 1999, after getting my passport, I went with Beau to Amsterdam, and I liked it enough that I started thinking about moving there. Part of the appeal of Amsterdam in particular was cannabis, which was not exactly legal there but was tolerated. Initially I thought "tolerated" meant you could just smoke anywhere, but I learned that that wasn't the case. There were specific places, mainly coffee shops, where you could smoke. I also learned that smoking cannabis and drinking alcohol were not done in tandem. It was one or the other, depending on where you were: coffee shops for cannabis, bars for drinking.

For a while I went to Holland on a regular basis, and I considered moving there. That went off the rails when they went from the guilder to the euro, because that immediately cut my retirement in half. I liked Holland because it had had African and Caribbean possessions, and when you went there and interacted with Black people, they would ask, "How come you guys are so racist in the US?" The white Dutch people asked the same question: "Why are you guys so racist in the US?" Then you'd go out to Rotterdam or something, which is like being in Oakland, and they're like, "You guys are so racist in the US." Rotterdam is like a combination of LA and Oakland. And then you cross over into Belgium, where they're like, "Well, we really like quiet people." They don't say they don't like you, but it's like, "We really like quiet people." The thing about Dutch society is that they've already mingled. You see kids that are my color, dark, with blond curls. White kids with Afros. You see all these extreme mixtures, and they make it work. I dig that. Because at some point, ethnicity doesn't matter. You ask them what they are and they say, "I'm Dutch." They don't say "Afro-Dutch." They say, "I'm Dutch." That's why I really liked Holland and felt comfortable walking around there.

Similar in Baja. I'd go into a bar in the local area, away from the tourist area, and they'd ask me, "Where are you from?"

"From the Bay Area," I'd say. "I'm here for a bike ride."

"That race with all the gringos?"

"Yeah, with all the gringos."

"Why are you here in the bar?"

"I don't hang around with gringos. I wanna hang around with the people who live here."

"That's good! What are you drinking?"

"Well, right now I'm having a Tecate."

"Okay, when you finish we have another one waiting on you."

I'd go there in the daytime, I'd go there at night. I'd walk back across town to Ensenada Boulevard, not a problem in the world. The white people are having issues, and they're only walking up and down the strip, on the other side of town. I made friends in Mexico that I was really comfortable with, and I don't make friends. They went out of their way to be extremely nice to me, not knowing who I was or what I was about. That was cool, because in Mexico there were no signals, no sign saying "Jonestown survivor" or "former Peoples Temple member." I was just a Black guy in Mexico who was treating them with respect, and they're treating me with respect.

In Amsterdam, I went to this restaurant called Haarlem, with two *A*s. Harlem in New York City is named after Haarlem. There's a Black woman in this restaurant and she's like, "This is really cool, where are you from?" I told her and she said, "Well, I'm from Los Angeles. My friend is from Atlanta, Georgia. We're opening up this restaurant." The Dutch don't know about Thanksgiving. She's like, "It's hard getting all the ingredients. Won't you guys come back?" We came back on Thanksgiving. The Dutch were loving it: the turkey, the cranberry sauce, the dressing. "What the hell is this? What do you call this?" We stayed until Christmas. They have an elf called Zwarte Piet, or Black Peter, who arrives on the Feast of St. Nicholas, December 6, and hands out sweets and presents to all the good children. He happens to be Black, either because he's an assistant to the Germanic god Odin who climbs down chimneys to spy on children, or because he's an enslaved demon. You see him all over town, like lawn jockeys. A lot of the people who pose as Zwarte Piet are white men in blackface. The Dutch explained him in a non-racist context. But now they're fighting about it, because it's derogatory. It made me realize that no matter what country you go to, there's going to be something. It's just a matter of whether it's a major or a minor something. That's a minor something, because the people are beautiful, and they're putting a positive light on a Black character. Here it's major, because in America people will kill you because of your color. And living in American society doesn't allow me the grace of being comfortable. What it allows me is to be in a position that my forefathers were not in: a position to defend myself, verbally if necessary, or physically as the last resort. Whereas for my forefathers, it was physical from the very beginning. They could not rationalize with their oppressors. "We're gonna fucking string you up," or "We're gonna kill you," or "We're gonna drag you," or "We're gonna tar and feather you."

There were people within Peoples Temple who had racist tendencies. And they weren't in a comfortable position, because if they showed their racism openly, they would be challenged openly, both physically and intellectually. Basically they saw Black people in positions of responsibility that they'd never seen Black people in. A white person from Indianapolis, Indiana wouldn't have been seeing Black people in leadership positions. That happened when they got to California and they started going to LA and San Francisco. And their racism got chipped away at over time, because in many ways Peoples Temple had become a Black church.

It was October 1999 when I made my first trip to Holland. Just a month earlier, in September, I had moved into the carriage house of a Victorian house built before 1900—the kind of house that many people think of as characteristic of Oakland. Those houses are actually prevalent mostly in two parts of the city: West Oakland, where the Black Panthers started, and the Fruitvale neighborhood, where Oscar Grant was shot. The Victorians are concentrated in those two areas because of commodities and transport: the Port of Oakland is adjacent to West Oakland, where refugees settled after the 1906 earthquake and fire in San Francisco, and the Fruitvale was where the railroads retrieved and delivered fruits and vegetables between Oakland and the Central Valley.

I had the opportunity to move into the carriage house because it was owned by the wife of a friend of mine and was just sitting empty. She had run a kindergarten there, but that had closed years before. I lived nearby and would visit them, and eventually I expressed interest in moving into it, if they could renovate it. It seemed perfect to me: It had an eight-foot fence and a stand of bamboo that gave me the sense of security and privacy that I needed, as well as off-street parking. It was almost like being back in the bush in Guyana. The sound of the wind in the bamboo was almost like the howler monkeys in the jungle, and it blocked street noise. It was 940 square feet not including the deck, and my rent stayed more than reasonable for the entire twenty years I ended up living there.

My landlords treated me like family, and the neighborhood was nice. But three or four years after I moved in, an unscrupulous landlord rented the house next door, as well as the duplex behind it, to a family of undesirables. The father was a heroin addict, and to support his habit he prostituted out one of his daughters. Their driveway abutted my outer wall, and there was a lot of noise as well as lookouts on the corners, watching out for police. A constant stream of people were coming and going at all hours, purchasing heroine, cocaine, and weed. I got fed up with all of this and, as a result, I became a member of something called the Neighborhood Crime Prevention Council.

The situation next door was intolerable. I felt it left me no choice but to become involved in community politics. Other neighbors were just as irritated as I was, but they were afraid to stand up. A lot of them weren't in a position to stand up because they were undocumented, despite having lived and worked in the United States for decades. As part of its initiative to address neighborhood crime, the NCPC had a program called National Night Out. It was already approved by the Oakland City Council to take place in as many neighborhoods as possible. National Night Out is, as its name suggests, a national thing, and it's still in existence. Its website defines it as "an annual community-building campaign that promotes police-community partnerships and neighborhood camaraderie." I signed up for our block in the Fruitvale district to take part in it.

The police brought a patrol car, and the fire department brought an engine. The kids were allowed to climb up on the engine and turn the siren on and were given little plastic fireman hats. They were also allowed to sit in the patrol car (and not in the back seat). While everybody was enjoying the fun activities and food, I introduced the adults to our local public safety officer, and he mingled up and down the street. He passed out his card, and people were encouraged to communicate with him anonymously if they had any problems. This was especially helpful to the families who had members who were undocumented. The National Night Out was a big success. Everybody showed up except the drug-dealing family and their cohorts—and we actually held it right in front of their driveway. Our message came through loud and clear: "We don't like what you're doing. We *all* don't like what you're doing." It got their attention, and things improved. Over a period of about seven years, we were able to clean that spot up.

My work with the NCPC and National Night Out led me to become involved with a police watchdog group called PUEBLO and with the Annie E. Casey Foundation, which works with at-risk youth. Annie E. Casey sent me to their headquarters in Baltimore to take some classes. Baltimore was eye-opening for me. I was a fan of the TV series *The Wire*, which aired from 2002 to 2008. The show was written by former *Baltimore Sun* police reporter David Simon, and it depicted things that were very similar to what I was experiencing and witnessing in Oakland: the way the city council operated; how certain neighborhoods were allowed to decay and were then bought up by speculators; how the police related to citizens; how investments were brought in to develop tourist areas—the waterfront in Baltimore, Jack London Square in Oakland—in lieu of supporting struggling communities. These things were being done in Oakland on the watch of Jerry Brown, who was mayor between 1999 and 2007.

In Baltimore I made it a point to go where *The Wire* had been filmed. I walked those streets and I saw those tenements. The similarities were eerie. I came back to Oakland and said, "Gentrification doesn't always work to your benefit. It can work to our benefit, but we have to be involved with the contractors. We have to be involved with the developers. We have to put criteria on them that they stay within this same model or style of building. They can't just put up this cookie cutter and leave these Victorian houses to waste away. They have to put up something that's respectful of that, or help us build these houses up so they're respectable." That didn't go over too well with community leaders.

All of this work led me to want to understand the police better: their motivation, why they over-patrolled some neighborhoods and patrolled others less or not at all, and how best to communicate with them. I wanted to be able to speak to the police in a language they would understand. The police are a two-edged sword. You can't live without them, but it's hard to live with them. And if you're living in the Fruitvale, or really anywhere in Oakland, you have to live with them. You study your adversary. So I studied the police. If you don't understand your adversary, you can't defend yourself against your adversary. You can't warn anybody about them, because you don't know how they work. The only way you can help young people is to help them understand the psyche of these guys, which allows them to maneuver around these situations. There's no need to get defensive. Explain the situation and stand your ground. There's no reason to get up and start yelling and screaming, because all you're doing is upsetting them, because they're by themselves. Backup is five minutes away. They're on their own. There's more of you than there are of them, typically. If you understand their psyche, it allows you to walk away alive, rather than being carried away dead.

I'm unusual for a Black man, because in my whole life I've only had three significant negative interactions with police officers. On a regular police check you won't see anything on me. But if you do a federal background check, different things do pop up, like the time I shoplifted in Fresno with my friend Gregory Hill. Gregory and I had grown up together on and off. He used to do tiptoe robberies. We'd done this many times prior. We'd go into a store, and he would actually tiptoe into the locker room or office and just pilfer, then tiptoe back out. He was Black in a white store, so he was seen as help.

On this occasion, I shoplifted a bicycle bag. I didn't know how to do it. I understood the tiptoe robbery, but I was just going to do a simple shoplift and get away. But I ran out of the store and threw the bag into a car to get it off my body, and when I threw it in the car, I woke a guy up. He woke up and yelled, "What the hell is this?" while I was being chased. He said, "Hey, this guy threw this bag in my car." So they took me upstairs and threatened me. They let me go but they said, "Don't come back to the store no more," and that was the end of it. I didn't go to Juvenile Hall or anything, and that was my last instance of ever even considering shoplifting anything. But it was a way of learning how the process goes, and also seeing just how adept Gregory was at these tiptoe robberies, which were beyond my expertise. I didn't even know there was a record of my shoplifting attempt, until I saw it in my FBI file. Everybody said, "You got a criminal record?" "No, I don't got no criminal record." But that's the only thing I've ever done.

Fresno's a very conflicted city. We lived on the west side, but we had homes, we had backyards, we had acreage, we had fruits and vegetables. The white kids lived on the white side. They had a front yard, they had a backyard. No fruits, no vegetables. That's kind of fucked up. They had a car, we had a car. I didn't feel less than my white counterpart, or that I had less. I felt that I had more than they did. I could come home and run barefoot in the dirt. They had sidewalks, their feet got burned. I could hunt, they didn't or couldn't. We could walk out into the country; ten minutes from my house we'd be out in the country. Those were all positives for me. I knew all my neighbors for blocks around. I didn't feel in danger when I walked up and down the street, no matter what time of day or night it was. Officers didn't come to our neighborhood. There was no reason for them to come to our neighborhood. Once I started going across town, that's when my mother warned me: "Don't show them any fear." I didn't get harassed then. There was racism there that I didn't know, because I was ignorant of it and had never faced racism, at least not overtly. Like I said, I didn't know I was Black until seventh grade.

As soon as Jonestown was over, I started graying at twenty-one. At thirty-five, I was pretty gray already. That might have thrown officers off to begin with. The only time while I was in Peoples Temple that I had an interaction with an officer was when Steve McIntosh and I were on the construction crew in Los Angeles, and we were walking down Pico Boulevard and cops pulled us over and said, "Where you going?"

"Going back to the Temple."

"Oh, you're the Peoples Temple boys." They make us get against the wall, they want to search us. Then they're grabbing our nuts and shit.

I said, "I hope you're enjoying yourself, because I'm not." When you're Temple kids, you think you're really fucking tough, but they don't give a shit about you. That was my first negative interaction with a police officer because I was in Peoples Temple.

After coming back, it wasn't police. It was FBI and other federal alphabet groups. And the FBI is a bit different from the police department, in the sense that, "We'll fucking take you in now, and nobody will know it." That's a lot different. I had plenty of friends who had negative interactions with police officers. It wasn't so much that I learned from their experiences, but I listened to their experiences as well as to what my mother said: "Don't show them any fear. They're like a dog. Don't show them any fear." I never have. And that doesn't mean that I'm all full of bravado and I have all this testosterone that makes me brave or whatnot. It just meant it was a definite instruction given by my mother, who had been raised under Jim Crow: "Don't show them no fear." She had seen riots, I suppose. I remember watching the riots in Watts and Detroit on TV as a kid, not really looking at my mom and seeing what her response was, but knowing that I was in Fresno and I was basically insulated from all that. There weren't that type of riots in Fresno. There were skirmishes in Fresno on and off, but nothing like that.

The City of Oakland participates in a national program called the Citizens Police Academy. It offered a fourteen-week course in all the different functions of the police department, as well as the responsibilities and functions of police officers. I was sponsored to take part in the Academy by Ignacio DeLafuente, a member of the city council. Once you graduate from the Citizens Police Academy, you're offered membership in CPAAA, the Citizens Police Academy Alumni Association. You have monthly meetings where you're able to communicate community problems to police leadership on a basis of equality and respect, and you function basically as a glee club for the police department. One thing we did was that, during the holiday season, along with uniformed officers, we would escort passengers coming off the Bay Area Rapid Transit (BART) trains from the station turnstile to their vehicles, so people felt they could shop in safety. The message was that the police department did more than just enforce the law; they were there to help the community. It showed officers and community members in partnership responding to community issues, rather than only reacting after something has already happened.

When I became president of the CPAAA, I told the OPD officers, "Look, we support you guys, okay? We're gonna support you. But understand, you have to support us too. If we're wearing this uniform with your emblem on it, you better damn sure fucking support us." That didn't mean, mind you, that I particularly cared for the OPD. But I wanted to know what it was about. Why are these kids being attacked? Why are these kids being shot? Why does it take so much longer for a patrol car to arrive in a neighborhood in the flatlands than in the hills, and why are the interactions so different? And one thing I found out was that the majority of OPD officers do not live in Oakland. They come in from Pleasanton, they come in from Tracy, they come in from Livermore. They come from Des Moines, Iowa, for that matter. There are many Black officers, but even the Black officers, once they become officers, move out of the city.

One of the requirements to graduate from the Citizens Police Academy is to go on a ridealong. I went on my ridealong and the officer says, "Well, we've got to go out to West Oakland." Okay. We go out to West Oakland, and he says, "There's some people out here in a car. Let me tell you what happened a few days ago. We found a white man in the trunk of his car, and the car was on fire." The man was from some place over in Marin County. "We don't know what the reason was for that, but now we got some other people out here in a car." We drive up, and he says, "You stay in the car." I'm in the car. He walks up at the ready, taps on the window, and this woman rolls down the window and he asks, "Would you please get out?"

You can see she's scared, but she's not trembling. It was a Black woman, and she's embarrassed. I'm thinking, "What the hell's going on?" He tells her, "See that car over there that's burnt up? We found a body inside that car just a few days ago." She says, "Look, my daughter moved back in." This was a year or two before the Great Recession, and the recession had already hit Oakland. "We don't have any privacy at home. This is the only privacy we got, is to come out here." Her husband's in the car, he's barefoot, and he's fucking mad. He says, "I can't believe this shit." The officer's trying to explain to him: "We're not harassing you. This is what happened. This spot is really private. We didn't want nothing else to happen." Then the man calms down and the woman is crying, because she's embarrassed. The cops have caught them in an embarrassing moment. The officer's like, "I can't tell you what to do, but this is too dangerous out here. Find another spot."

The officer was white. We leave there, we drive through downtown Oakland, and we're going to go to Pill Hill, where all these little pharmacies and little doctors' offices are located at. Before we get there a guy calls and says, "A guy just broke into my car." A car turns in front of us. The officer throws on the light and pulls it over. I'm out of the police car at this point; the officer hadn't told me to stay in. The guy's a Mexican national. It's him, a girl up front with a baby, and two guys in the back. They pull the female separate and have her stand by herself. There's screwdrivers and shit all over the floor.

"Let me see your driver's license." It's a Mexican driver's license. "You know this is not legal in America." The officer is talking to the girl and finds out that she's on parole. She had her baby behind bars, and she's only been out a couple of months. The baby's four or five months old.

The officer says, "Look, you either tell us what's going on, or you're going back to jail and your baby's not."

She says, "They're breaking into cars."

"Okay, you can go."

He lets her go. They call the paddy wagon and arrest the three guys.

Now I looked at that, and one side of me was saying, "Well, that's a sensitive moment." That was kind of cool. I probably would have done the same thing. But I wondered what these guys are going to do to the girl after the fact. "You ratted us out." Again, we go back to how women and children start the revolution. A woman's protecting her child. That's her responsibility, no matter what the fuck you guys are doing. She might have paid for that; I don't know. It gave me some insight into the dynamics of how these officers work.

Now, they might have been extra nice because I was there, who knows. I can't say one way or the other. I just know that they treated this lady with respect. It's a scenario that could have gone ape shit, because they could have come out with guns blazing. Another time I was with OPD, and we're in the neighborhoods. I was working with the Annie E. Casey Foundation. And the officer tells me, "You know, in the old days I'd just come back here after work, out of uniform, and give them a little tune-up. Can't do that anymore, but that's what I'd do in the old days." These guys felt comfortable saying things like that to me. It's like, "You would, would you?"

One odd moment was that they had these Belgian Malinois dogs, like a scrawny German shepherd but they can climb. They can climb a chain link fence, just like you would climb a chain link fence. They can also climb trees. It's $10,000 or more per dog, including purchasing it as a puppy plus all the specialized training they need. I'm with the K-9 unit, and they're telling me funny stories. They send this dog in: "Go." The dog's in there searching. They know the guys are in there. They're waiting for the dog to alert them. Five minutes pass, ten minutes pass. What's going on?

They come in cautiously, they go through the house, they finally make it to the kitchen. And there's a pizza on the floor, and the dog's eating the hell out of the pizza. The guys are gone, and they've been gone. This is a $10,000 dog, and it gets sidetracked by a pizza. They said, "You just never know." The other thing is that these dogs are so trained that if they're given the command to go after you and you give them the alternate command to stop, they'll be in midair and just stop. When I see these guys in Ferguson or in Baltimore, and the dog is going off and they can't pull him off, they're not trying to control the dog. It's not that they can't pull the dog off—they won't. They're purposely giving that dog a command, and the dog's acting on it, but because they're on camera they're doing all this shit, but they haven't given the command to stop. Sometimes some agencies train their dogs, and the commands are in German even though they're in America, and that gives them an alternate command.

The thing that puts the OPD in a predicament is that they're supposed to have 1,100 officers minimum, for a population of 360,000. The actual number of officers fluctuates. We've had it as high as 900 and something, but in the twenty-plus years I've resided in Oakland they've never had a full contingent. As of September 1, 2020, they had 747 officers. What that means is that when an officer goes out, he's by himself. He has to wait for backup. Either he cajoles the people, or he gets the most aggressive ones and pulls them to the side and arrests them because they're being so aggressive. The problem's not solved, but it allows them to leave.

It was important for me to understand all these things for my own survival, as well as for the young people I was around in the Annie E. Casey Foundation, because there were a lot of young people coming in off the streets. It wasn't that they were having issues with the police, but they were reaching an age where they wanted to speak out. When young kids speak out, they scream and sometimes yell profanities. They yell what they think will get to the officer. But the fact that you stopped and didn't run got to the officer. The fact that you asked him, "Why are you pulling me over? Why are you stopping me? What is your reason?"—that stymies them immediately. "I need your badge number and your name. I'm not answering any questions without a lawyer. I've done nothing. You've got no reason to arrest me, and if you do, I have nothing to say. I'm taking the fifth." Now, it doesn't mean you won, but it allows you to fight another day. It means you survived. You lost the battle, but you win the war. And I was trying to get that through to these young people I was working with.

I wanted to understand the Oakland Police Department because one particular year, I forget what year it was, there were a lot of shootings, well over a hundred shootings in Oakland. Cops would get involved, and they'd have their shootout. It just kept escalating and escalating. It didn't make sense to me.

It calmed down later, because they put in more community policing. Community policing allows you to have a safety officer. You call the safety officer: "Hey Joe, this is Eugene, I'm at such-and-such address. Can we meet or can we talk later on? My neighbor's mad, they're going off, they're doing this." The safety officer goes over to their residence. "Hey, we aren't getting a complaint, but it seems like you're disturbing your neighbor. Can we get both of you guys together and let's talk about it?" That alleviates that tension, because when you're in a cage, whether it's a physical cage with bars or a territorial cage, meaning that you can't go past this block and you can't go past that block, at some point you have too many rats in the cage. They fight each other. If somebody from the outside has to come in and temper that, typically that's a police officer.

Do you want your uniforms doing psychology, or do you want to have an officer specifically geared towards that, a public safety officer who's been versed in that and understands conflict management? Your average officer is not interested in stopping the conflict. They just want to go on to the next issue. "Can you guys get along, yes or no? If not, I'm taking somebody in." Conflict finished. Done, but it's not. I go out the next morning, and I go back next door and whoop his ass again. Nothing's been solved. With a conflict management person, such as a public safety officer, it doesn't eliminate that, but it does alleviate it by opening a line of communication: "Can you two get along? If you can't get along, we'll have to figure out why. Whatever the common interest or concern is, we'll work from that." A public safety officer is almost like a therapist.

Oakland is an odd town, because there are more renters than homeowners. Renters vote in the moment, rather than voting for their future. When they vote in the moment, it's against the landlord. "I don't like my landlord, I'm voting against them." But they're voting against their own interests. But because it's emotional, they don't see it. And when an officer shows up at their apartment, versus at a house they might own, they're treated much differently, and they don't understand why.

I saw what was happening to my people. Not to me—what was happening to my people. That was part of what had led me into the political side of what Peoples Temple was. The Temple allowed me to act out without getting in trouble. It allowed me to be part of an organization that was speaking out against injustices, without the risk of being singled out as an individual and put in prison for it. I knew that, no matter how much I argued and fought and did whatever I did in the Temple, basically they weren't going to let anybody drag me away. It's a brazen statement now, but in that day it was a fact, because everything was handled internally. We're not going to turn any of our members over to police officers. That's a strength as a young Black man that you have to take advantage of: knowing that you can speak out and resist and revolt and know that you have hundreds of people that will support you. They might kick your ass after the fact, but publicly they're on your side.

And some of those people were white. They were allies. In the Temple I had plenty of white friends as well as plenty of Black friends. My protectors were white, although those that defended me were of color. Jack Beam was at the height of the hierarchy, so any problem would get handled immediately. Black men and women that were further down, or lateral, also came to my defense. Rheaviana Beam, Jack's wife, took a liking to me. Ruby Carroll took a liking to me. Anita Ijames took a liking to me. Lee Ingram took a liking to me. Don Jackson took a liking to me. Multiple people supported and protected me, and I don't know why. I quit asking, but I learned to accept and express my gratitude. I quit beating myself up about why. They all taught me something. They all gave me gifts that lasted all my life.

I always observed. That's just force of habit. I observed, and I made mental notes: Don't do this, don't do that. Make sure you say this, make sure you say that. I had some interactions with police as an adult, like the one in LA. Most of my interactions were with the FBI. Local cops didn't really fuck with me. But it's about what they're doing to my people. Not me, my people. Those who are not the ones being beaten have a responsibility to speak up about what's happening and make it known.

PART THREE

BACK TO THE WORLD

CHAPTER 9
Small World

Around 2001 or 2002, I'd been transferred up to Sacramento to write up some type of safety thing within Caltrans. I'm working with this beautiful sister, Lisa. We're talking. Whenever I think I'm going to like somebody or I want them to be part of my life, I tell them about the part of my life that's horrible. If they're willing to accept that, it means they're willing to accept me, and I definitely will accept them. So I tell Lisa my story.

As luck would have it she goes, "Hey, things happen. But you know what, I know somebody else who was there."

I said, "Really?"

She says, "Yeah, he works over at the Department of Agriculture."

"Really?"

"Come on, we can go over there."

So we're across the street from the state capitol building, and we leave the Department of Transportation and walk over to the Department of Agriculture. I walk in, and she says, "This is Eugene Smith." I look at this man, and it's Odell Fucking Rhodes.

This is the same man that was the reason I got held in Georgetown longer after November 18, because this specific man said I was part of the hit team and that I had been instructed by Stephan Jones to bring the plane down and make sure there were no survivors. Odell was in Jonestown proper on the day, when the murders and suicides were happening, and he escaped through the bush. Once I had been told that and then read it years later, I had an animosity towards him. I'd always been mad at him because, when he escaped, he didn't take any children with him.

So I'm looking at him, and I'm containing myself, because I should jump across this fucking desk and bang his head as many times as I can into that desk until he's a pulp. I said, "Hey, my name's Eugene Smith. I'm glad to meet you." We played it off like we didn't know each other. Lisa didn't know. So we're talking a few minutes and I said, "Well, we gotta go. Hope to see you again." He waves off to me.

For us to actually know the same person, and for her to introduce us to each other, was uncomfortable for me. It's a small world. I come back the next day by myself and I say, "Man, I know you know me. I know you. Lisa knows about me. She knows about you. Don't fuck up my relationship with her."

He just sat there. There was some fear there, but not overt, just like shaking in his boots kind of fear. That kind of fear you get when somebody has caught you, and you're wondering what the discipline is going to be, and they never discipline you. It's like, "When is it gonna fucking happen? When is the other shoe gonna drop? The first one's already in my ass." We left it at that.

Odell joined Peoples Temple in Detroit during one of its cross-country bus trips, along with another guy named Curtis. I think they were both living on the streets then. Odell had sustained an injury in Vietnam, and one of his legs was shorter than the other. He had this primitive little odd gait when he walked. He was always a good communicator. He was for the most part dedicated. He went to Jonestown in August 1977, during the first wave of the Temple's migration, eight months ahead of me. He worked with children there, like he had done stateside.

I never worked with children very much, other than showing them how to do something or how to build something or how to tear something down. I didn't interact with the children that much. It just wasn't in my scope of responsibilities. In the Temple, Odell seemed dedicated, in the sense that he was there for the cause. I didn't see him as trying to play a game. He brought his street wits with him. "This gets me by. This gives me another day. This allows me to have some enjoyment. This allows me to be a normal person and not live on the streets or anything." He did what was necessary to do that. He wasn't as brazen or bodacious as I or some of my friends were, but he came in under different conditions. We were pretty much introduced and brought in. Whereas he came in, in my opinion, like "Fuck this, I'm escaping Detroit and the streets and I got a meal. Yes. Cool. I've arrived." With that comes a certain level of responsibility, or a certain level of debt. You've done this for me, I'll do this for you. Somewhat like Chuck Beikman. Not the same, but similar.

Odell and I didn't run in the same circles. By the time he joined, I was already established.

At Jonestown there were a thousand people. You might know a couple hundred of them, which means there's eight hundred you don't know. It's just like society. You come across people on the bus or train that you catch every day to work. You know them, but you don't. You know their name for that moment, but if somebody asks you, "Hey, do you know Gary?"—well, you catch the bus with him every day. Stuff like that. And after November 18, there were sets of survivors. All those sets didn't know why the other sets survived. Jones had already set up this circle of paranoia, saying he had his "avenging angels." Well fuck, who's an avenging angel? Anybody that survives is an avenging angel. That was already set up years in advance. He always said, "You'll never escape me. I'll always have angels out there that you don't know of." It was the way Jones hid some of the defections and unexpected departures.

That's not to say that these people did take vengeance or anything. But since they weren't there to defend themselves, and chose not to defend themselves when they came back, all you're going on was Jones's word: "This is my avenging angel. The only people that can leave are the ones that are truly trusted." Which wasn't the fact. A lot of people were able to leave because he was fearful of them and their personality traits. And who knows what Jones was saying in the days before November 18? And for all Odell Rhodes knew, the quote-unquote basketball team might very well have been a cover, and I might have been assigned to make sure the plane was shot down with no survivors.

I had gotten fingered for something I wasn't part of, and then, to meet the person who had fingered me, twenty-plus years after the fact, it brought back everything. It made everything very present again. The people who escaped through the bush, they were at one hotel in Georgetown. The ones that were on the basketball team were somewhere else. Those of us who were at Lamaha Gardens on November 18 were the largest contingent. And we had the shortwave radio, which is how Sharon Amos received the order to kill herself and her children. So I could understand them being fearful of us. But when things get made up about a person, that's not right. And the person in question in this case was me. People have made mistakes and said things they shouldn't have said. But who would've thought that the US government would go to the degree that it did to make sure that these people would be ostracized, to a point that they'll never be trusted by anybody ever again?

I couldn't show my anger to Odell in front of Lisa. I didn't need him reacting. I needed him responding to me but not reacting to me, which is why I waited another day to have a private conversation with him. "I know you know me." But it went fine. I got my point across. I couldn't imagine how infuriated he might've been, as well. Lisa put us both on the spot. But she was proud: "Oh, I know somebody else who was there."

I never saw Odell Rhodes again. I transferred back out of Sacramento down to District Four of the Department of Transportation, which is located in Oakland. Odell passed away in 2014. His son got in touch with me through Lisa. She asked me to call him, so I called him. He wanted to know about his dad. The son was an okay guy. I don't know if he was born after, or what. I didn't know anything about him. The thing is, I wasn't even interested in learning anything about him. I guess he had never met his father, or only knew of his father, or only saw him when he was a child or something. You don't destroy that. You just let it go.

CHAPTER 10
Stepping Out

Sometime in the late summer of 2004, a playwright named Leigh Fondakowski contacted me via my friend Fielding "Mac" McGehee. Mac's wife, Rebecca Moore, lost two sisters and a three-year-old nephew in Jonestown. Mac and Rebecca have devoted themselves to documenting the good, the bad, and the ugly about Jonestown, Peoples Temple, and Jim Jones through their website *Alternative Considerations of Jonestown and Peoples Temple*, a digital archive housed at San Diego State University. Leigh Fondakowski had been the head writer for *The Laramie Project*, a play about the torture and murder of the gay teenager Matthew Shepard in Wyoming, and her next project was a play about Peoples Temple. When she asked Mac who might be willing to speak to her, he included my name on his list.

So Leigh called me and told me, "There's a play that's gonna be at the Berkeley Repertory Theater, and I just wanted to get things straight." The play was in fact complete—I think the actors were already in Berkeley rehearsing—but she was still doing research. She hadn't talked to someone like me, meaning someone who came into the Temple from the outside. I said, "Okay." What impressed me was that Leigh and her collaborators wanted to show a timeline, from observing Jones, to joining Jones, to representing Jones. What people don't realize is that it was all normal, until it became abnormal. And that initial normalcy was what allowed people to join the Temple with a whole heart. So Leigh told me, "I've got a friend that lives in Oakland, my cowriter, Margo Hall." I said, "Have Margo give me a call, maybe we can meet." A few days later Margo came over to the house and said, "Look, you have a responsibility, because we haven't heard from any other Black men." That caught my attention, because Margo herself was Black. A white person could not have convinced me in the same way, because the agenda is different, and they could never see my story through my eyes. But when Margo told me I had a responsibility, I took it to heart.

Two years earlier, in September 2002, I had become fully tenured in my job at Caltrans, with ten years of service. That meant that I could never be fired except for just cause, and that I was already entitled to a partial pension if I were to retire. At twenty years, I would be entitled to a full pension. This kind of security was exactly what I had planned for years earlier when I began looking for a government job. Caltrans was the job that came along for me in 1992. The other thing getting tenured meant to me, emotionally, was that I finally felt like I was an American. Until then, I didn't feel I was entitled to anything that I had worked for. After cataloguing the assets of Peoples Temple after the mass murder-suicide, the court-appointed receiver was giving cash payouts to survivors. I would have been entitled to one of those, because I lost my mother, wife, and son at Jonestown, but only if I admitted that I had been programmed. I wasn't willing to admit that. They were also offering therapy, and I said to them, "If I was programmed, I wouldn't know that I needed help." So I turned them down. And it was only twenty-four years later that getting fully tenured in my Caltrans job made me feel fully secure and fully American.

Getting tenured also meant that I wasn't going to have to work for the rest of my life. And it meant I didn't have to be friendly to anybody if I didn't want to. I didn't have to make friends unless I chose to. I wasn't looking for friends; all my friends had died. And now I was tenured in my job and guaranteed a pension from the State of California. And those things put together meant that another thing I had was freedom. So I cooperated with Leigh Fondakowski and Margo Hall, and they ended up including me in the play. There was no longer any reason for me to hide anything.

A few weeks after I did my interview with Margo, Leigh sent me transcripts of most of it, with highlighted text that she wanted me to check and okay for use in the play. With the transcripts she included a letter. "I cannot begin to tell you how significant your interview was to our process," she wrote. "Your story will have an immensely positive impact on our play. Your memories are so distinct, your story-telling so clear. It's not only the clarity with which you tell your story that's important, but the perspectives and insights you hold are like no other material we have."

Margo told me that I was going to be portrayed in the play by a Black actor named Colman Domingo. "He's a really good actor," she said. "Do you mind coming down to the theater and just talking to him and the other actors? Because you knew all the people who are being portrayed in the play." So I went to the theater in Berkeley and talked to the actors as a group and then talked to Colman Domingo one on one. My motivation was that I needed him to have my personality. I needed him to be a little bit arrogant, but still to have some compassion. I needed him to understand the character he was portraying. I told him about my childhood in Fresno, how I kicked Terry Trovato's ass after he called me a nigger, how I organized a walkout on Martin Luther King's birthday in ninth grade in 1972, how I got kicked out of Fresno High and then forged my mom's signature so I could get into an all-Black high school. I needed to get him up to speed about all these things that happened before I got involved with Peoples Temple. And what I needed him to understand was that Peoples Temple gave me an opportunity to be a revolutionary and to have support. Once I was inside I saw the disparity, the clashes, and the racism within the Temple. But at that time, the good outweighed the bad.

He took it all in. I remember that he took copious notes. That didn't sit well with me; it put me on alert. But then I reflected that if I had been playing him, I would have done the same thing. So I calmed down and eased into it. He was a Black man from the East Coast, from a very different background from mine. We had nothing in common other than this play. But he was a character actor, a good one, and he understood that his job was to become the person that he was portraying. He didn't seem shocked at all by the things I told him; he took everything in stride. I gave him pieces of my personality, and he took it on. I told him, "What you have to understand is that the majority of the people were not there to support Jones. They were there to support the ideals and the other people who were living those ideals. You didn't want to desert them, so there were things you would accept that you otherwise would not have accepted." I told him that I had done a short stint of security for Jones when he met Jimmy Carter in San Francisco, but that I would never have taken a bullet to save Jones. I would have taken a bullet to save my wife or my child or my mother. I wanted to go down fighting. Colman Domingo and I met more than once during the first half of April 2005, just before the play began its run. They were holding full rehearsals of the play, and I was able to comment on those.

The play was my introduction to the world, and specifically it was my introduction to the hundreds of people that I interacted with at the California State Department of Transportation. I had one particular officemate there who was rather talkative. In my estimation he took liberties, like assuming we were friends. For me friendship comes over a period of time, after you've faced things together, and I've never tried to form friendships at work because you're in a controlled environment there and you never know what the friendship is based on. I think he thought that because he was Black and I was Black, that was all that was necessary to have a friendship. One day we were having a conversation, and he mentioned that he had a son with an ex-girlfriend, and his current girlfriend had a couple of children. I said, "That's nice." And then he asked me did I have any children. I said no. And then he said, "Why not?" And I said, "That's really none of your business." It infuriated me, because the implication of what he was saying was that all Black men have children, and you're not a man unless you have a child.

I remember finishing off the day and going home and thinking about it. And I had to go over to the Berkeley Repertory Theater, and I told Leigh about it. I told her, "These are the kinds of things that you face from society when they don't know your story." So I said, "I want that in the play." It was an innocent moment, because I don't think my coworker meant to hurt or to be malicious, but his ignorance superseded his common sense. Leigh went for it, and they put that encounter in the play.

A few days passed, and the play was about to debut. And I said to my coworker, "Hey, they're making a play, and I'm one of the characters in it. I've got some comp tickets. I'd be honored if you and your girlfriend would attend." He said, "Sure, when's it gonna be?" I said "Saturday" or whatever, and he said, "All right." I actually wasn't sure whether I was going to attend the opening until the day itself. I had no qualms about the play overall, but it was just difficult watching somebody walking and talking like me. But I did end up attending the opening. And my officemate was there too. The next time I saw him back at work, he said, "Hey, how come you never told me?" And I said, "You never asked." He said, "Well, I didn't know what to ask." And I said, "Exactly. So you shouldn't have said nothing. When I said I didn't have any children, you should have just left it alone." That was a tense moment. After that I was able to continue working with him comfortably enough, but I kept my distance.

I ended up attending the play itself maybe twice. Several times I just took part in question-and-answer sessions in the afternoon, and also just to observe the audience. I liked seeing how people's thought processes went. There was one lady, a Black lady, who attended one of the Q-and-As. She raised her hand, and Leigh called on her. I was sitting directly behind the lady. And she launched right in: "They were all crazy. They were programmed. They were following a sinner." Her implication was that all Peoples Temple members were guilty by association, whether they survived or not, and that ministers and church members didn't have any duty to respect them. As she's going on, Leigh is looking at me, and I can see the whites of her eyes. Her mouth is agape. She's looking at me like, "Please, Eugene." The lady went on for maybe four or five minutes. She never really asked a question; she just gave her five-minute commentary. The half dozen or so people who spoke after her were either neutral or positive. And after it was over and people were leaving, Leigh came up to me and said, "Eugene, I'm so sorry, I had no idea this was gonna happen." I said, "Don't sweat it. It's no big thing. People are entitled to their opinion, right, wrong, or indifferent." But I said, "What it does show is that in some factions, nothing has changed since the day of the incident."

A couple weeks after the play opened, on April 30, there was an open invite for survivors and family members to go to the California Historical Society in San Francisco, which was the repository for Peoples Temple's effects. I hadn't known there was a repository. So I went over there and one of the volunteer archivists, Denice Stephenson, whom I had met previously at the Berkeley Repertory, showed me some binders of photographs. Denice was working with the lead archivist, Mary Morganti. Denice got into the Peoples Temple thing and stuck with it for a few years, and she compiled a book of some of the most important Temple documents called *Dear People: Remembering Jonestown: Selections from the Peoples Temple Collection at the California Historical Society.* I looked at the photos and told her, "That's not who that is." She said, "Are you sure?" I said, "Yeah." And over the course of a few hours, I said, "A lot of these are misidentified. These people aren't who they say they are. Can I come back?" Denice said, "Sure." And I said, "I'll come back on the weekend and help you out with these. A lot of these people are misidentified, and that's not fair." I was the only person in the Bay Area that was willing to do that at that time. Part of my motivation was that I thought I might come across some photos of Ollie. I think a lot of people had the assumption that all the information at the historical society was correct. But I knew that it wasn't.

The archivists—Denice, Tanya Hollis before her, Mary Morganti, and other CHS staff—hadn't known anyone in the Temple and didn't know they were making mistakes. Often all they had were sheets of individual photos from the Temple's files, with names written on the back, and they assumed that each name corresponded with the photo on the flip side of the sheet. Often they did, but sometimes they didn't. The mistakes the archivists made were honest ones, but they were still mistakes and needed to be corrected. The inaccuracy was understandable because of the quantity of material that they had. They already had five or six thousand photographs from multiple sources. Some of them were duplicates. Different people had made conflicting identifications, and many photos had no identification at all. Around this time, the widow of a reporter donated another four or five thousand photographs. So I came back in May and started working with the archivists on weekends. I spent the rest of that year identifying people in those photographs, until the historical society staff said, "That's enough, Eugene."

Going through all those photos and clippings was a release in a sense, because I had actually forgotten a lot of people. Or rather, I had forgotten who was there and who wasn't there. And after so many years or decades, you forget who's dead and who's alive. Going through all those photographs and stuff allowed me to go, "Oh okay, oh good, they're still around," or "Oh, I forgot about her," or "I forgot about him." The pictures were of everyone: people who died, people who survived, people who had been members and left. Some weekends were good, some were bad, but overall the experience was more positive than negative.

Because the play had come out, I was ready to face whatever fallout there might be. I just didn't have any fear anymore. And it worked to my benefit. I had reached my crux in terms of "I can deal with it now financially, I've already survived the worst, I'm comfortable enough with myself that I feel confident that I can survive this as well." When I was younger, in my twenties and thirties, there would have been no way. It wouldn't have happened. But now, I took my chances. It was nothing tremendous or anything. For me, it was common sense. And it was just time. And people had become willing to listen to more than one type of narrative. It seemed like the American public had become open to hearing not so much an alternative story, but an additional story, to go along with the one they had heard. That there were normal people there. That not everybody was a maniacal weirdo. So at that point, I didn't have anything to lose. Earlier, I had had everything to lose. I would have been risking my livelihood, not to mention my sanity. I had to concentrate on seeking employment and a roof over my head, on finding and maintaining stability. But once I was vested after ten years in my job with the State of California, I felt secure enough to start talking about it. And I was willing to defend it legally if necessary, because my record of work was outstanding.

The play was a success. It has been staged in a dozen theaters across the country, including the Guthrie in Minneapolis and the American Theater Company in Chicago. Leigh took the success and expanded it into a book, *Stories from Jonestown*, which included more perspectives of survivors than a two-hour play ever could. Colman Domingo, who portrayed me, has also gone on to success, with scores of acting and directing credits on stage and in television and film, including in *Ma Rainey's Black Bottom*, starring Viola Davis and the late Chadwick Boseman, released at the end of 2020.

In 2006 a documentary was aired on PBS called *Jonestown: The Life and Death of Peoples Temple*, directed by Stanley Nelson. I ended up being in that too, and in a similar way to how I had ended up being portrayed in the play. Late in the process, with the film almost completed, Mac McGehee of the *Alternative Considerations* website encouraged Nelson to interview me. We talked on the phone, and then he asked me to meet him at a house they had rented in the Berkeley hills. He explained that they needed to be in a quiet area so there wouldn't be as much background noise during filming. So I showed up, and if you watch the film, the blue shirt I'm wearing is actually one that I purchased in Guyana. I deliberately wore it for the film, because if I was going to relive it, I had to be in the moment. Initially Nelson's questions seemed softballish to me. But after watching the documentary, I could see how he needed to bring the audience along.

I think *Jonestown: The Life and Death of Peoples Temple* had merit. Nothing had been done on Jonestown to that extent previously, and even now it holds its own. It won awards at the Tribeca Film Festival in New York and the San Francisco International Film Festival, and it was short-listed for an Oscar in the feature documentary category. Its influence has been positive. The Kool-Aid jokes didn't cease, but the film offered its viewers multiple narratives from people who had *been there*: in Jonestown, in Georgetown, in San Francisco, in LA, in Redwood Valley. What viewers maybe didn't realize was that they were seeing different sets of survivors, different rungs on the ladder. Overall, I think the film was well done, noteworthy, and ahead of its time.

Mac McGehee was also excellent about vetting media personnel when they came to him expressing interest in writing about Jonestown or Peoples Temple. I liked the fact that he would vet them first before sending them to me, because that gave me freedom as well as more time to spend with them. If I had had to vet them myself, I would have been neither as diligent nor as cordial as Mac was. I wanted the media to interview me, because I wanted to put a different narrative out there, but at the same time I despised the media because of the narrative they had been putting out there without verification or due consideration of forty years' worth of research. I had to sort out the ones who wanted to tell a story from those who just wanted to sell a story. But doing that sorting out was hard work, especially for someone like me who was already skeptical of their biases and motives. I would always do my own little bit of vetting, but Mac would do the heavy lifting first, which I appreciate. By the time reporters got to me, they were well prepared to be careful and deferential, and they knew what not to ask. What I wanted was for them to feel as uncomfortable as I had felt while the FBI and CIA were interrogating me at JFK Airport in December 1978. When reporters get too comfortable, they go off script and start asking inappropriate questions out of their own personal interest. I needed them to stay on point.

Mac was also the person I approached for help getting my Freedom of Information Act file from the government. He got that for me, and that piqued my interest in learning what else the *Alternative Considerations* website does. And what it does is give survivors, former Peoples Temple members, and relatives a safe environment to ask questions and get answers. "Did you know my uncle? What was he like?" Questions like that, as well as larger questions about the politics of the Temple and the reasons people joined. It was through *Alternative Considerations* that Odell Rhodes's son ended up approaching me to learn about his father, for example. The website also gives survivors and family members an outlet to tell their own stories, as well as to read about people they wanted to know about but didn't necessarily want to meet. Finally, the digital archive presents a wide array of perspectives on Peoples Temple and Jonestown from a multitude of divergent, often contradictory, viewpoints. It has a different kind of value than the material held by the California Historical Society. The historical society has a great many documents, photos, and memorabilia, but the SDSU project gives you a more complete picture of the people of Peoples Temple, both living and dead. As I got to know Mac and his wife Becky better and became familiar with the work they were doing, I was really impressed.

Over the decades, many books have been published about Peoples Temple and Jonestown. Many of the early ones were done by reporters and shock jocks and Temple apostates, writers who were more interested in sensationalism and their own opinions than in accuracy. There have also been quite a few memoirs published, although for some reason none before now by a Black man. I've never read any of them. The reason is that I don't need to read somebody else's rendition of my life. I don't want to be poisoned by misinformation. And I don't want to forget my memories or intersperse my memories with the memories of others.

I own a library of roughly eighteen hundred books, of which only five concern Peoples Temple, Jonestown, and Jim Jones. Denice Stephenson gave me her book *Dear People* as my parting gift for helping her identify photographs at the historical society. Judy Bebelaar interviewed me for her book *And Then They Were Gone: Teenagers of Peoples Temple from High School to Jonestown*. Judy was a teacher at Opportunity High School in San Francisco, and many Temple teenagers, including Ollie, had been among her students. She gifted me a copy. I have a copy of *San Francisco Examiner* reporter David Talbot's book *Season of the Witch*, which covers Bay Area politics in the 1970s, because I was on a speaker's panel with Talbot at the historical society, and he signed the copy that I had bought used. During our panel I corrected him about something, and he inscribed my copy, "Thank you for spreading the truth." I have a copy of a memorial album of portraits by Kathryn Barbour, called *Who Died on November 18, 1978 in the Jonestown, Guyana Mass Murder-Suicides*. Kathryn is a former Temple member who was in San Francisco on November 18. She's the kind of person who, when she gets her teeth into something, can be obsessive to the point of blindness toward everything else around her. "This is all I know; this will come to fruition." In the Temple she was haughty toward many people, but she was always communicative with me. For some reason, she took time for me.

The only other book I have is *The Road to Jonestown* by Jeff Guinn. Whenever a book on Jonestown or Peoples Temple is published and the author speaks at the California Historical Society, I make a point of showing up, so I can either critique them to myself or compliment them privately after their talk. I went to hear Jeff Guinn speak, and he earned my respect because he had actually trekked through the jungle in Guyana to see what was left of Jonestown, despite being up in age. Where the compound used to be is all overgrown now. Jeff used to be the books editor of the *Fort Worth Star-Telegram* newspaper. When I introduced myself to him, he said, "Your story needs to be told," and he promised to speak to Dan Williams at TCU Press as soon as he got back to Texas so that could happen. Other than the picture book *Who Died*, Jeff's book and the one by David Talbot are the only two that I've actually purchased. I'm simply not really interested in most of the more than seventy other books on Peoples Temple and Jonestown, not counting novels and poetry, because how can you write a book if you weren't there?

CHAPTER 11
Remembering and Forgetting

Sometime in 2007, my girlfriend Tina and I were down in Orange County, visiting her mother. I hadn't spent time in Southern California in forever and a day. I had only driven through it to get to Mexico. I really didn't like Southern Cal, and I had left Compton to return to Fresno in 1979 with a bit of a brick on my back. Not a boulder, but a brick, and I never went out of my way to go back there. But this visit to Tina's mom got me thinking about J. W. Osborne, my mother's friend who had taken me in when I showed up in Compton on New Year's Eve 1978, straight from LAX after being flown by the feds from JFK. So while we were down there I called the house and Utte, J. W.'s wife, answered the phone. It was Utte who had said "I love you" to me through the door when I told her it was me, back in 1978.

Now, when she answered the phone, I said, "Hey, Utte, it's me, Butch."

She said, as only a Black mother can, "Hey baby, you okay? How you doin'?"

"I'm okay," I assured her. "I'm down here in Orange County. I was thinking of dropping by the house. Is J. W. home?"

"Oh." I heard her hesitate. "Why don't you just come on by?" She didn't answer my question. I just assumed he had been an ass, or acted the fool, and there might be some tension there, but it was okay. I told her Tina and I would be there in a couple hours.

On the way there I explained to Tina who J. W. Osborne was in my life: that he was my mother's best friend, that he had given me a place to stay when I first came back from Guyana, that he had introduced his daughter Lisa to me as my sister. In my young man's mind I hadn't thought much about that, because being adopted, I had a lot of people who were extended family to me.

Utte greeted us at the door and she was the same loving, affectionate, caring person she had always been. We sat down on the couch. It was one of those couches from the seventies, with a plastic cover on it. I remember thinking, "Wow, some things never change." And Utte said, "Lisa'll be here in a minute or so. She has something to tell you." And I thought, "Well, this'll be interesting." The last time I had seen Lisa, she had been a child.

So Lisa comes in. "Hey, big brother, how you doin'?" And she gives me a big hug. There's a doorway, and she's standing partially in the living room and partially in the hallway. And that's when she and Utte told me that J. W. had passed away about a month earlier. And I thought, "Well, at least the two of you have peace." Because J. W. had been a weekend drunk and verbally abusive. That was my thought, but I didn't vocalize it.

And then Lisa said, "I've got something to tell you."

I said, "Okay."

She said, "I'm your sister."

I said, "You've always been my sister."

And she said, "No. Really your sister."

I said, "Okay. What do you mean?"

She said, "J. W. was your father."

I said, "How do you figure that?"

"He said, 'They killed my son over there.' He was talking about you." She was referring to the period between November 18 and New Year's Eve 1978, when he thought I had died in Jonestown. And that made me wonder how he knew that I had been in Jonestown. The only way he could have known was that my mother must have communicated with him somehow.

So I said, "Wow. Excuse me. I love you both, but I really need to get back to the Bay Area. I need to think about this."

I had hours to think about it on the drive back. Learning what I had just learned gave me reason to hate J. W. Osborne. Before, I had disliked him, I was irritated by him, but I was grateful. But now, I hated him.

After the deaths at Jonestown, it took seven months for most of the bodies to be buried. Many remained in Dover, Delaware, unclaimed and unidentified. But the other reason for the delay was that no cemetery wanted to have anything to do with them. Finally, Evergreen Cemetery in Oakland agreed to accept them. There was a service when more than four hundred bodies were interred there in May 1979. Beginning on the first anniversary, there have been memorial services every November 18 led by Rev. Jynona Norwood, a Southern California minister who lost a large number of family members in Jonestown. In more recent years there has been a second service at Evergreen on November 18, organized by Jonestown survivors and former members, away from the cameras and press that cover Rev. Norwood's service. And in 2011, the Jonestown Memorial Committee, a small group of survivors and relatives who had come together for the specific purpose of erecting a memorial to the Jonestown dead listing all their names, succeeded in its efforts. A service of dedication was held in May of that year.

For many years, I never attended any of the services. I still hadn't gotten past the rage I felt toward some of my fellow survivors. I thought that, if I had been in Jonestown on that day, I would have challenged what happened, I would have fought to the bitter end. But I didn't know that. I couldn't know that. I wasn't there, so there's no way of knowing what I would or wouldn't have done. It's clear that some people who were at Jonestown did resist, because some were found with injection marks between their shoulder blades. But I felt an unbridled rage, which I could keep under control only by riding motorcycles fast and not attending the commemorations. Until the fortieth anniversary, I think I had been to two of them.

The only reason I even entertained going to them in these later years was that my rage had subsided. Forty years is a long time to stay mad. These days, I communicate with Jimmy—Jim Jones Jr.—on average maybe once a year, Stephan maybe twice. Usually it's through something else: "Oh, hey man. How you doing?" Or there's a funeral. It's weird to attend a funeral with people with whom you share a death. But I was asked to speak at the fortieth anniversary commemoration in 2018, and I met with Stephan and Jimmy the day before that.

Not attending the commemorations all those years was a choice, because I loved these people, but at the same time there's a certain electricity that happens when we're all together in the same room. It's not positive or negative, it's just a certain electricity that I pick up on. Now, I enjoy seeing the people. Some have done good, some have done not so good. It's always good to see them in a positive light. But being around them is very, very stressful because of what we've gone through, and what some are still continuing to go through. I said, "It's not that I don't care or I'm insensitive. I just don't want to be around y'all, because it's difficult." It's not even about old memories or anything. It's just feelings, emotions, validation of decisions made. Some were good, and a lot were bad. It's also validation of mistakes made. It's validation of a lot of good things that happened in my life, but also validation of every bad thing that happened in my life. I feel conflicted when I see my fellow survivors, so I don't make a habit of it.

But in 2018, it was shared with me that they wanted this to be an uplifting anniversary. They didn't want it to be doom and gloom, even though what we're going through now is doom and gloom. They wanted it to be a happy moment. But life never ends on a happy note. You do things, but you end up dying. And you might do a happy thing, but it ends with you dying, and that's not a happy note. I wanted to be as truthful as possible. I wanted people to feel good about themselves and about what they heard, but also I needed them to know that we were in the most dangerous time of my lifetime, other than the time we had already gone through on November 18, 1978. We could be happy that we were now into our senior years, but we had lived long enough to see history repeat itself. That's nothing to be happy about, and I'm not surprised by it. What we have to be happy about is that we're still here, and we're still fighting the negative narrative. What I enjoyed most was that, forty years after the fact, people could see that we survivors were a representation of America, and that we were all different. The only thing we agreed on was that you weren't going to come for one of us without coming for all of us. I think that's something to be proud of, and that we can live with that.

I felt that the two years between November 18, 2018, and November 3, 2020, might be the second most dangerous period of our lives. All Americans were being put in a position where we were having to make choices that we had never had to face before. Were we going to be the people we were raised to be? Were we going to treat people the way we wanted to be treated? Or were we going to follow this mob mentality, where an outspoken few just want to wreak havoc and cause disruption and distractions and diversions that are injurious to all of us? Those are hard choices for people, because if you're not affected by it directly, why get involved? That's how it was in 1978. A lot of things wouldn't have happened had more people been involved, had more people spoken out, had more people said, "This needs to be investigated," had more people said, "Something seems wrong here, we should look into it." Just like in recent years people have justified other people getting beat up or run over by a car, like in Charlottesville, or shot in the back, like in Ferguson. "Well, you know, he shouldn't have done this, he shouldn't have been there." It's justifying a death because it didn't affect you personally.

The 2018 commemoration was going to take place at Evergreen Cemetery, as usual, but it was going to be different, in the sense that there wasn't going to be the usual doom and gloom. I was told it was going to be about celebrating the fact that we had survived being survivors. In 1978 I had been twenty-one; now I was sixty-one. We hadn't been expected to live. It just wasn't going to happen. It's like I survived twice. I tell people I survived November 18, I died on the twenty-first, then I was reincarnated on the twenty-second. This is my second life. Sometimes it's overwhelming, and other times it's really passé in terms of what actually happened. Things have stuck with me that I'm really glad I didn't forget. There were a lot of reasons to forget. I understand them. I've spoken to a lot of people more in the last decade than I spoke to them the whole time I was in the Temple and they lived one room down from me.

There were sets of survivors. There were Jonestown survivors, there were Georgetown survivors. Two people going down the Kaituma River on the *Cudjoe* were survivors. One person was in transit from the States and arrived in Georgetown on the night of November 18, to hear on the radio about the assassination of Congressman Ryan at the beginning of the incident that killed her two children; she survived. There were people who were preparing to go to Guyana, who had just sold their homes and given up all their possessions to leave, sitting at the Temple waiting for their number to roll up. They got to the airport and went back. It broke thousands of hearts. The collateral damage is unimaginable. Some people gave up their children so their children would have a better life over there, and it was the ultimate mistake. Your children shouldn't die before you do. When they do, you carry guilt. You have a guilt that can't be explained, other than that you failed. I'm not a failure type of guy, but I failed that.

There were things that were happening in the Temple that I knew were happening, but they weren't affecting me directly. To a certain extent you accept things, thinking that's going to be better than fighting immediately. When you're in a triple canopy jungle, 250 miles from the closest metropolitan center, which isn't that big anyway, things become a whole lot more serious. You engage immediately. And I still think that's part of the reason I was sent out of Jonestown to Georgetown: because I was engaging, and I wouldn't be quiet anymore. I think I showed my resentment physically. I think I showed that, "I'm fucking tired of this, this doesn't make any sense." I thought Jonestown would be a jumping-off point and that the young folks would either go to Cuba to be in medical work or be revolutionaries and fight causes worldwide. I didn't see me making twenty-five. I never had any doubt. I knew I wasn't going to make twenty-five. My son would, but I wouldn't. Ollie would be fine, but I wouldn't make it. I knew that. I knew that positively. I presumed that they would be okay. But it actually turned out the opposite of what I had in mind.

When you lined up for dinner at Jonestown, to get your meal you had to greet the servers in three different languages: Russian, Chinese, and maybe a Spanish or Cuban quotation. That's forced indoctrination, but what it does is, it trains you to accept something. You must eat, but in order to eat, you must comply. It's an indoctrination, subtle, but there just the same. Showing resentment of that showed them that I was definitely not going to go another step further than that. I think that might've been part of the reason they said, "You need to go to Georgetown for a while." I was protective of my child. Even in California I had shown my willingness to challenge them, which is probably why I had come to Jonestown with the last group.

In October 2018, as the fortieth anniversary approached and these things were on my mind, I posted a piece on the *Alternative Considerations* website that I titled "Not Surviving Jonestown." I wrote:

> The year 2018 is an odd year with an even number.
>
> Forty years have passed so fast, yet at the same time, they have dragged. There are folks I haven't seen in 41 years, and there are others I see on an irregular basis. This anniversary is a moment in time as well as timely. We've all matured and have become

individuals, versus being lumped together as "members" of Peoples Temple.

I see November 1978 with completely different eyes now in comparison to what I saw then. I aged 40 years in a single week. Now 40 years later, my body has caught up to my mind and eyes that saw so much when I was 21.

What's odd is that I feel younger in my mind now than I did at 21. Life is a funny and sad journey. Here I am at 61, retired, less tolerant of bullshit but understanding that when it comes to life, it's necessary to live it rather than exist and accept.

I am no longer ashamed of Jonestown, but I am deeply saddened and haunted at times. I'm happy that some years I have forgotten the anniversary date when it passes, but haunted by the fact that it happened and I was defenseless to change the outcome. I have moments of guilt that destroy my soul for days at a time. I look back on occasion and see Ollie, and I think of how I failed at the most basic responsibility of protecting her. I look back at my son, whom I barely recall and cannot remember what he looked like. Some years I forget both of their birthdays. I don't have any pictures of them. All the ones I had were with my mother in Jonestown. None were ever returned.

All I have are memories, remorse, guilt, and moments of elation followed by unbridled anger. Part of that anger stems from my realization that the world at large doesn't get it.

The difference now is that I realize that the majority of so-called *survivors* were traumatized teenagers and young adults who were expected to come back to a society that shunned us in 1978, and that still stares at us in 2018. We never meant any harm to the USA. All I wanted was to be treated as an equal and allowed to grieve openly. Neither happened then. I'm not sure whether it will happen now, 40 years after the fact. I'm not sure it will ever happen.

The media wants our story every year or so, especially on the anniversaries. They ask sometimes, they demand at other times, they want the story not yet told to be told just so they can get it before any other media outlet does. Never do they ask, how can I help you for sharing this? How are you doing?

> None of us survived Jonestown – none of us – because the world ended on that day. What we did survive was returning to the United States and being criticized for 40 years, getting a job, restarting a family, being an asset to society, helping children, joining community organizations, fighting individually for civil rights for all. We're still alive, but we did not survive.

You can watch the speech I gave at the cemetery on November 18, 2018, online if you really want to, but I'm not going to talk about it here. What the American public picked up from all the media coverage of Jonestown, and what it has continued believing all these years, is, "Don't forget how crazy those people were." That's what I take offense at. I resent it, although I do understand it. Not only are we not forgiven, but we haven't been forgotten about either. And the thing is that the perpetrators didn't survive, but we survivors are treated as if we were the perpetrators.

I don't want the American public to forget the tragedy that happened at Jonestown. I don't want them to forget the steps that were taken that led to it happening. I don't want them to forget the lessons learned from that. What I want them to forget is the people that survived. That's all we did. We just survived. That's it. Forget us. Don't forget the incident. Don't forget the person that perpetrated it. Don't forget the individuals that allowed it to happen. Don't forget the politicians that pretty much put the stamp of justification on it. They're forgiven. Like Jerry Brown. Like Mervyn Dymally. Movie stars, like Jane Fonda. They call her Hanoi Jane, but they never pulled back the Peoples Temple part of that on her. So I'm telling them, "Can't you forget us?" That's all. I want to be forgotten. The irony is that I'm writing a book so that you'll remember.

And it's not so much an embarrassment as it is a disappointment, because Peoples Temple could have been much, much more. It could have set an example, not for Americans to leave the US, but for us all to have a better life here, by sharing. That's it. Really simple. And right now we're in a society that says, "Don't share shit. Get what the fuck you can and hold on to it. Get as much as you can, and even if you've got enough and you're satisfied, get more just in case." And we're going to put you in a position to where you're not going to be able to share because you're not living, you're only surviving. You've got just enough money to make it to your next check, get some food, and pay your bills.

The societal aspect, in my opinion, is that they got tricked. They went down there. They got killed. The ones that survived just got lucky. The other aspect is that they went down there for a noble cause, but they followed the individual rather than the cause. They killed themselves based on somebody telling them to do it to themselves, rather than saying, "No, we're not gonna kill ourselves. And whatever's happening, we're gonna stand our ground."

A lot of people say that they followed the Devil, that Jones was the antichrist. "They perished. It was good. It's the best thing that could have happened. If they had come back to the US they would have poisoned the whole United States, or at least they would have poisoned that crazy-ass Northern California. How can we trust them? They survived for a reason. He told us there were going to be survivors. He told us there would be avenging angels, people who would take vengeance. The survivors are them." Those are the extremes. But it's not extreme if you have hundreds of thousands, if not millions, of people thinking the same exact thing. That takes it out of the realm of extremes, into the realm of possibility. What people forget is that, at twenty-one, I was an old survivor. There were some survivors that were up in age, but just a few. The majority of us were between fifteen and twenty-four. And over the years since, we've done nothing criminal. There are no arrest records. We haven't started a new organization or anything. The people that wanted to start a new organization are members that didn't go to Jonestown, who wished they had gone but didn't. "We need to start this again." I'm like, "Get the fuck outta here."

America and the media want us to explain why Jones did what he did. We don't know. That's what I told the Guyanese interrogators in Georgetown, and it's what I told the FBI and the other alphabet agencies at JFK. And it's what I'm telling you now, more than forty years later. We can't explain it, because we didn't know and we still don't know. If we had known, believe me, for all the shit we've been put through, I would have told you. I didn't even know about the incident until three days later. I have a response, but I don't have an answer to why he did it.

Jones didn't like being alone. He liked to be able to have access, to be able to travel and do whatever. When he thought he couldn't leave Jonestown, even to go to Georgetown without being arrested for violating a California state court order in the child custody case involving little John Victor Stoen, I think he felt hobbled. Jonestown was his refuge, but it was also his prison. What he thought about his prison, what he thought about the people he increasingly tried to control with intimidation and discipline, why he thought the deaths of a thousand people would release him, I don't know. I don't know what his mindset was. And the reason I don't know what his mindset was is because I'm not a madman.

For me the fortieth anniversary was the beginning of the end, and the writing of this book, the telling of the tale, is the end. It's the end because I'm cleansing my soul. It's the end of me having to discuss this, to defend this, to debate, to explain. I hope this book does that. Over more than forty years since that day, I've done nothing to embarrass my family, my wife, my son, my mother, my grandmother-in-law, my friends, my associates, my buddies, my ace coon booms, my enemies, those I didn't like, those I cared about, those I loved, those I hated. I've done nothing malicious to embarrass them. That is something to be happy about. And the system hasn't found any reason to arrest me, stymie me, cripple me, or imprison me for any of my thought process or anything I've been involved in. That goes for all of us, because when we came back we were all on the list.

The fact that we made it means that we've got a lot to be happy about. Doesn't mean we have to be proud. Doesn't mean we have to jump for joy. But we have something to be happy about, something to be proud about. That day will never be forgotten in American history because, actually, it was a day when more than nine hundred people took a stand for what they believed in. Somebody might say, "Yeah, but they were killed, they were murdered. Some committed suicide." Yes, but they took a stand first. The end result was different, but the initial thing was that they took a stand for what they believed in and said, "I'm willing to live elsewhere. I'm willing to move, I'm willing to leave. I'm willing to say, 'Fuck you,' and give up my citizenship to do so." As long as we're still here, we survivors, and we still have our voices, we can tell the stories that undermine the prevailing narrative. By us being here, there's always an objection to what the media is going to say. Since we're here, we're still alive, we still have our voice, we still have our strength, we still have our intelligence, we can debate that. Not only can we debate it, we can debate it vigorously and with fact.

Survivor's guilt really simply is: I survived, he, she, or they didn't. Why did I, and why didn't they? Three or four days after the incident we knew that everybody was dead, and it was like: Why did I live? I didn't do anything special. You start doubting what your skillset is, and who you are, and that you're even deserving of life. Then you look back, and you see adults and children who never had a chance, and never would have a chance, and you saw this greatness in them, and it's gone. And then you see people you've made friends with over the years, people you consider mentors or confidants, or you consider more intelligent than yourself, or people you can get advice from, and you survived and they didn't.

Coming back to the US, back to the world, I've lost my family, everything that represents me, everything that I am, everything that describes me or says, "This is Eugene Smith." All of that is destroyed or gone. Everything I put my effort into is destroyed or gone. My promises are destroyed and gone. My dreams are destroyed and gone. My wants and needs are destroyed and gone. What is the purpose? What's the reason for continuing on with this journey? It's not like, "Well, I can just start over." When you lose your world, you don't feel like that. All of us, not just me, we all lost our world that day. I remember family members coming over to Guyana or trying to get to the airport, and there'd be newscasts like, "Well, how'd they get out and my mom didn't?" or "How'd they get out and my dad didn't?" or "How'd they get out and my sister didn't? How'd they get out?" It's like, "Who are they? How come they lived?" Then you're saying, "I don't know," which is the worst thing to say. The Guyanese didn't like it when I said it. Family members didn't like when I said it. The news media didn't like when I said it. My own family didn't like when I said it. The FBI certainly didn't like it. But I really don't know.

I don't know if it was an operation. I don't know if it was a plan gone wrong. I don't know if, for all intents and purposes, it was a set design to get rid of the best. Because there were some truly gifted people over there, gifted in ways you can never imagine. Gifted in policy, gifted in skillset, gifted in language, gifted in negotiation. Gifted in a multitude of kinds of expertise that were just lost. Expertise that wouldn't have helped only Peoples Temple, it would have helped the United States. It would have helped the world. It's like they took the cream of the crop and said, "You're gone." Then you survived and it's like, "Well, fuck, am I the cream of the crop?" No. They killed the cream of the crop. Now I'm tasked with having to either be a complete fuckup, so nobody ever pays any attention to me again, or to be everything they couldn't be. In any case, I came back with a level of responsibility that obligates me not to embarrass them. I'm not going to embarrass Ollie. I'm not going to embarrass Martin or Christa or my mother. I'm not going to do anything that would cause them embarrassment, or bring embarrassment upon Jonestown. Not because of the name, fucking Jonestown. Because of the people that were in Jonestown. I owed every single one of them, whether they were friend or foe. I cannot embarrass them. I came back with that mindset, and it allowed me to navigate life and not kill myself, because suicide is an out. Some people commit suicide because they can't take it anymore. Some people commit suicide because they're just tired. Some people commit suicide because it's the better of two options, living through this shit day after day or just calling it a fucking day and being done with it. That's not to say that suicide is easy; it's to say that not all the people in Jonestown committed suicide. A lot of them were murdered.

Those that were murdered, I have to stand for. I think everybody that came back had a feeling about specific people. That they would do it—commit suicide—or they wouldn't do it. I don't think my mom ever could have come back to the US. I feel it's highly likely she committed suicide. I think quite the opposite of Ollie, because Ollie was my completion. She was my controlled anger. And Martin meant more to her than anybody—more than her mother, her sisters, me, anybody. Martin meant more to her than anyone, and she would not give up on him. That's how I feel. It might have been different, but I won't believe that. When you listen to Tim Carter talk about seeing his wife inject the poison into his baby's mouth, I can't comprehend that.

When we were living on Buchanan Street in San Francisco, before we went to Jonestown, there was a period when Ollie wanted to leave the Temple. And I convinced her to stay. Then there was a period when I wanted to leave, and she convinced me to stay. She was having issues with her mom. "Your mom beat you," I said to her. "Your mom abused you. You can't go back home." Ollie's grandmother was already in Guyana, which I didn't really know until I was there. Again, what does that go back to? It wasn't Jones. It was people. It was individuals. Her grandmother, my mother. We're indebted to them. So it wasn't all this la-la, pie-in-the-sky shit.

So it is convoluted. It is confusing. It is didactic. It is conflict. It's all of that. But that's what made it so dynamic. In a certain sense, the madness was what made it operate. The madness was that if you give people a promise, and they see that promise exemplified in individuals, they'll accept more than they would normally accept, because of the promise that's physically real. In other words, I promise you this is going to be fantastic. Yeah, right. Whatever. Then you see this person over there that was a junkie six months ago, and now they're a model citizen. So the promise is physical now. You do that dozens if not hundreds of times, and hundreds if not thousands of people see that, and you now have a movement. And the bullshit and the nonsense seem to be part of what makes it work.

And the rest is history. It's a simple equation. People make it complicated, but it's fucking simple. There's nothing complicated about it. It's human nature. Jones understood that. When you came into Peoples Temple, people sized you up. You had hundreds of conversations. If you had a conversation with a hundred people during the week, thirty of them were studying you: "What makes him tick?" It's all about human nature and exploiting that. Exploiting normal human weaknesses. Not weaknesses because you've been beat down. Quite the opposite: weakness because you've been built up. My weakness that they exploited was that I was loyal to my family in times of crisis, like the FBI said about me afterwards. Jones and the echelon knew that, when push came to shove, I put my loyalty to my wife, my child, and my mother over my loyalty to them. So I got removed from security positions early on. "He's not gonna fight for us." And they were correct. I wasn't going to.

It's thoughts like these that haunt me, anger me, hurt me, stymie me, and have made it impossible for me to trust. On the other hand my experience has made me very aware, less tolerant of bullshit. And I take nothing for granted, ever. I hold survivors to a much higher standard than I do society at large. Society has the excuse of ignorance about who we are and what we were all about, we who saw, experienced, and lived through many lovely times, punctuated by a few moments of unbridled violence for a so-called belief.

So, I survived. So now what?

CHAPTER 12
Listen to the Record

Having as much past in you as I do, and not being able to say anything about it, ages you. In an interview I did with the *Guardian* around the time Leigh Fondakowski's play came out, I said, "I feel freed of the past now." I feel the same now, having written this book. And now I'm giving myself the freedom to forget.

When I first came back stateside at the end of 1978, I listened to a small number of record albums on a regular basis. One was *Whatcha See Is Whatcha Get* by the Dramatics, especially the song "In the Rain": "Once the sun comes out/ And the rain is gone away/ I know I'm gonna see/ A better day." The feelings that song evoked in me were intensified by how much it actually, literally, rained in Guyana. The Dramatics allowed me to take my anger and hold onto it just a little while longer. Gil Scott-Heron was the prophet. He released an album with Brian Jackson in 1975 called *From South Africa to South Carolina*. His album *Winter in America* is self-explanatory: "Ain't nobody fighting 'cause nobody knows what to save." I still have all his LPs in my garage.

And then there was Curtis Mayfield. He was the messenger. His song titles say a lot: "Move On Up" from his debut solo album *Curtis* (1970), "Keep On Keeping On" from *Roots* (1971). *Super Fly*, which he's best known for, came out in '72. But the one that really spoke to me was *Back to the World* (1973), whose title song is about a Black vet returning from Vietnam. It's about the Black experience of going to a foreign country and killing people who never called us niggers or did anything against us, and doing that in the name of the United States of America, and then returning to the streets of American cities. "The war was never won."

Like that vet, in 1979 I had just returned from a war, and I was facing another war at home. Americans felt we survivors weren't worthy of forgiveness; they had us labeled as fanatics and didn't want anything to do with us. I was coming back to a society that I had renounced, but I had nowhere else to go, so I had to swallow my pride and get on with my life. I was coming back to where I was from, America, so whether I liked it or not I was coming home. I had left the States because it was a nightmare here, but I went to Guyana and survived a nightmare there. And now that I was back home, I had to make some decisions. I could fight, or I could forget about it, or I could remember every fucking thing I could and write about it one day. But first, I had to survive. I had already survived long enough to get back here—back to the world—but now it was going to be about surviving survival.

Forty-plus years later, I'm seeing the same things being repeated all around me, like a broken record. Again now, people are stepping back and saying, "Oh, I don't want to be involved. I'm just trying to live my life." Well, it's kind of hard to live your life in society without affecting somebody else's life. Now we as a country, or we as citizens, or we as survivors, are faced with a choice. Are we going to speak out, which we know how to do? Or are we going to be silent?

Here's what I mean by a broken record: New Year's Eve and the Fourth of July are murder days in American cities. People shoot people, but it's covered up by all the fireworks and everything. Someone can get killed, but the body not found until twelve hours later. So I tend to stay close to home on those days. And when a young Black man named Oscar Grant was murdered on the platform of Fruitvale Station in Oakland by BART Police after midnight on New Year's Day 2009, I didn't so much react to that killing in particular, as much as I was feeling, "This stuff has to come to a fuckin' head." I lived only seven blocks from Fruitvale Station, and what I remember is that people were stopping cars in the street, and the BART trains wouldn't stop at Fruitvale. That incident later became well known because of the dedication of Grant's uncle and then the movie *Fruitvale Station*, starring Michael B. Jordan and Octavia Spencer. There's a lot of local history in that movie, but it came out almost four years after the fact. Oakland is always tense, but until it's brought into public view it just keeps going and the cops keep escalating. Oscar Grant was only one in an unending string of fatal incidents, just another straw added to the camel's back.

There had been so many killings throughout 2008 in particular that it had almost become normalized. In Oakland alone, at least sixty-seven suspects were shot by OPD officers between 2000 and 2012. On March 14,

2008, a seventy-one-year-old man named Casper Banjo was shot and killed after pointing a toy gun at OPD officers. On April 26 of that year, twenty-one-year-old Andrew Gonzalez was killed while fleeing after crashing a stolen car into a police cruiser. Charles Griffin was killed by cops while fleeing on August 22. So the killing of Oscar Grant was a tragedy, to be sure, but it was only one of many. And it was soon overshadowed by the poor handling of the pursuit of Lovelle Nixon on March 21, 2009, that resulted in his death and those of four OPD officers. Oscar Grant was an exemplary young man, by all accounts. Nixon, on the other hand, did kill two cops unprovoked, and he was a convicted felon and had committed a series of violent rapes. But the cops turned him from a criminal into a hero. OPD is notorious for doing that.

Oakland in recent years has been at a low boil. Now it's about to boil over, because it's having to make decisions it's never made before. You have Silicon Valley moving in, you have San Francisco moving in, you have people from Marin County moving in, you have people from Southern California moving in, and they're all high tech. They're coming in with massive amounts of money. They're not interested in integrating. They're interested in conquering. "I want my coffee shop on every block. I want my convenience store"—a certain kind of convenience store. "I don't like Safeway, I like Whole Foods. I don't want people walking around all times of night. They can walk until ten o'clock, and after that I want the streets to be quiet. I don't like them celebrating their holidays, I want them to celebrate my holidays, because they're in America now." The problem with that is that I live in America too, but they celebrate the Fourth of July and I celebrate Juneteenth.

The social media site Nextdoor was initially dominated in Oakland by white people who had moved into Black neighborhoods. It was their way of communicating with each other: "My next-door neighbor looks suspicious." He's been there twenty years, they've been there twenty days. And the police would respond to that shit. And people were like, "I've been here twenty fucking years, she hasn't been here a fucking month, and you're harassing me like this?" The notorious Barbecue Becky incident of April 29, 2018, just happened to be caught on video. White people were calling police on kids riding skateboards on the sidewalk on the other side of the street. Incidents like that by the dozens. It got to the point where they actually shut down the Nextdoor website and said, "No, you can't do this anymore. You must identify who you are, where you live, what your address is, if you want to post your complaints against people." Because Black people were rightly saying, "They come in here, they're visitors, and we're the ones that are being harassed."

All of this has brought Oakland to the verge of upheaval. And it's going to be about classism. Racism is part of that, but classism is different, because now I affect your livelihood. Racism affects you in terms of living and dying, which affects your livelihood, because if you're dead you can't live, obviously. But when it comes to classism, it's like, "Well, I brought a business with me, but I'm not hiring anybody like you. In fact, I'm gonna make sure you don't get hired." That's classism. It's a racist ideology, but it's classism because it's like, "I'm not gonna allow you to make this money to move up this ladder. I'm doing it because I'm personally offended by you, because you make noise where I don't want you to make noise."

Around 2018 we were having ICE raids almost daily in Oakland, and they were not being reported. There were Mexicans on my street. In 2018 they were there on a Friday, they were happy. By Monday evening the house was empty, all the shades were open, the doors were locked, the cars were gone, and they never returned. And the house stood vacant, no For Sale sign or anything. That family's son was a US citizen, but the father wasn't. He was here on a visa. The son was working with Doctors without Borders. So I saw firsthand the effect that bad immigration policy has, not only on an individual and a family, but on a neighborhood and its cohesiveness. Oakland has become a battleground, although it's a quiet battle. Wars or conflicts always start quietly, because it's all about messaging. The messages are being put out that "We're coming to town, we don't appreciate you being here. Not only that, but the land is cheap and we want it, and we're willing to pay more than what you can pay for it, so they're gonna sell it to us."

There used to be a radio station in the Bay Area called Quiet Storm that played smooth jazz and rhythm and blues. Smokey Robinson made an album with that same title. What's happening is a quiet storm. A quiet storm is a conflict that starts with words, but at some point it goes past the verbal and even the political and becomes physical. When that happens, Oakland is going to be something to be reckoned with. Everybody thinks the Bay Area is this liberal bastion, but it's really not. It's being corroded away. It started in the eighties and has escalated in recent years.

In the mideighties, there were multiple hangings of Black people at and near BART stations. "Oh, that was a suicide." No way. Back then they didn't say out loud what they thought. Now, they tell us *why* they hate us. "*This* is why I hate you." They don't hold back. They've reached a comfort zone, and they're not afraid anymore. They've become brazen. Drivers in the Bay Area are among the most aggressive drivers in the country. So what I'm saying is that it took a long time to get here, but it's here. In my opinion, what they want is armed warfare.

There's a certain segment of the US population that is at war with people of color. They're at war to the point where they're killing us without provocation, and our response is to march, and protest, and write letters. As Malcolm X said, ballot or bullet. And the choice we're going to have to come up with sooner rather than later is: Is it going to be the ballot, or will it be the bullet?

Something has to change, and it has to change drastically, and it has to affect enough people to where we can make a positive change. As long as it's segregated change, we'll never respond to it as a whole. And what are we survivors going to do? Are we going to help the rest of the United States survive with us? Or are we going to be survivors again? The positive thing is that we don't have to agree with everything, or with anything. We don't even have to like each other. But one thing we have to agree on is that we all want to be treated like human beings, and that we want everybody else to be treated like human beings, and that we have a responsibility to do that.

As I've said on the *Alternative Considerations* website and in the previous chapter, I hold Jonestown survivors to a higher standard. We've been here before, and we know the truth. We know how bad it can really get. Now, that's not to say that there's going to be a mass suicide throughout the United States. But it is a death by a thousand cuts. They'll shoot somebody in Chicago, they'll shoot somebody in LA, they'll shoot somebody in San Francisco or Oakland, they'll shoot somebody in Ferguson, they'll shoot somebody in New York. They'll strangle somebody with their knee in Minneapolis. Individually it doesn't affect you, but collectively, they're killing off a generation. And that's what happened in Jonestown. They killed off a generation. They killed off multiple generations. I don't want to say "They," though. Multiple generations were murdered or committed suicide rather than come back and face what was happening then in the United States, which is the same thing we're facing now. The only difference is that there is no escape from this. There's nowhere to go. That means that we have to stand our ground. You can stand your ground in multiple ways. It's not my intention to instruct you on how to stand your ground. I can't tell you how to do that. But I do tell you that you must do it.

Jonestown was a microcosm, an experiment in a society being controlled, and in how far the control could go before people resisted. When that point came, that's when Jones pulled out his trump card: the Flavor Aid. The phrase "drinking the Kool-Aid" has long been current in American parlance, and I've always hated it, but over the past few years, and especially since the coronavirus pandemic began, it's been in vogue. These days everybody is getting a dose of Jonestown, whether they like it or not. This is the first time in modern times that Americans have been controlled in this fashion from outside their households by government entities. You're being forced to be a socialist, whether you want to be one or not. The people who are resisting what needs to be done for everyone's good are the ones that have a fascist streak.

It's irritating to me that, four decades later, like a broken record, we're going through all this all over again. It's corrosive, it's toxic, it's depressing, it's bewildering. What was the point of going through everything, just to end up with this result, which is a non-result? Do we have a death cult? Who's the nut? Where's the cult at? Who's the cult leader? Back then, they drank Flavor Aid. Today they're drinking chloroquine and injecting disinfectant and refusing to wear masks.

Wouldn't you like to get back to the world?

APPENDIX

My FBI File

As the saying goes from back in the day, just because you're paranoid doesn't mean they aren't after you. With help from Fielding McGehee of the *Alternative Considerations* website, I used the Freedom of Information Act to obtain a copy of the full file kept on me by the Federal Bureau of Investigation. It turned out to be more than three hundred pages long, and it amply confirmed my suspicions about their suspicions about me.

Their harassment of me is comprehensible—if not excusable—if we understand the mentality that US officialdom had toward Peoples Temple as a whole. Of course, it didn't help that Jim Jones was, especially toward the end, genuinely a megalomaniacal madman.

The never-solved murder of Chris Lewis, which I mention in Chapter 6, is one case in point. A memo to the director of the FBI with the subject RYMUR (the acronym refers to the murder of Congressman Leo Ryan on the airstrip at Matthews Ridge), dated 12/28/78, reads in part:

> For the information of the FBI Laboratory, CHRISTOPHER LEWIS, Negro male, date of birth 9/24/43, a former member of the People's [sic] Temple, San Francisco, California, was shot and killed on December 10, 1977. Removed from his body and from the crime scene were the enclosed projectiles.
>
> Through information developed in the San Francisco Division concerning the assassination of Congressman LEO RYAN, there have been allegations that the People's Temple may have been responsible for numerous criminal acts, including the murder of CHRISTOPHER LEWIS.

More dramatic than that is the claim in a teletype sent from the secretary of state of the United States to FBI headquarters on 12/1/78:

> REFERENCED TELEGRAMS AS WELL AS NEWS MEDIA COVERAGE CONCERNING THE GROUP KNOWN AS THE 'PEOPLES TEMPLE' HAVE STATED THAT THERE MAY HAVE BEEN OR INFERRED THAT THERE MAY STILL EXIST A PLAN TO ASSASSINATE THE PRESIDENT OF THE UNITED STATES AND ALL IN LINE OF SUCCESSION, OR TO ASSASSINATE/KIDNAP HIGH RANKING GOVERNMENT OFFICIALS.
>
> THE DEPARTMENT OF STATE, OFFICE OF SECURITY, HAS THE PROTECTIVE RESPONSIBILITY FOR SECRETARY OF STATE CYRUS VANCE. TO MEET OUR RESPONSIBILITIES, IT IS REQUESTED THAT THE DOS, OFFICE OF SECURITY, BE NOTIFIED IMMEDIATELY OF ANY INFORMATION REGARDING THE SECRETARY, HIS OFFICE, OR ANY DEPARTMENT OF STATE EMPLOYEE, DURING THE ONGOING INVESTIGATIONS BEING CONDUCTED BY THE U.S. SECRET SERVICE/FBI.

In his memo passing this on to his staff, the director of the FBI added:

> ANY OFFICES IN RECEIPT OF INFORMATION CONCERNING A THREAT TO SECRETARY OF STATE BY THE PEOPLES TEMPLE IMMEDIATELY ADVISE FBIHQ SO THAT STATE DEPARTMENT CAN BE ADVISED.

Another page of my file includes this assertion:

> BQMRA IN RECEIPT OF TELEPHONE CALL FROM (X) [Redacted] (X), A PASSENGER ON PAN AMERICAN AIRLINES FLIGHT 228, WHO ADVISED THAT PT MEMBERS HAVE PLANS TO REGROUP IN THE UNITED STATES AND ARE DEFINITELY ANTI GOVERNMENT.

As I wrote in Chapter 2, in January 1979 I had to make a special trip from Compton to San Francisco, where I stayed overnight with my friends Steve McIntosh and Pumpkin, just to tell the feds again, this time in court, that I didn't know any of what they thought I knew. Also in my FBI file is this:

> [Redacted] was presented with a subpoena to Testify Before Grand Jury in the United States District Court for the Northern District of California by Special Agent (SA) [redacted] on December 29, 1978. [Redacted] is to appear in the Grand Jury Room, 17th Floor, 430 Golden Gate Avenue, San Francisco, California, on January 24, 1979, at 9:30 AM.

This also apparently refers to me:

> ON NOV 28, 1978, [redacted] ADVISED THAT IN THE LATTER HALF OF 1975 HE ATTENDED A PLANNING COMMISSION (PC) MEETING OF THE PEOPLE'S TEMPLE (PT) AT THE TEMPLE IN LOS ANGELES. HE STATED THAT JONES AND ABOUT 40 OTHER MEMBERS WERE PRESENT. DURING THE MEETING A HANDWRITTEN NOTE WAS PASSED AROUND FOR THE VARIOUS MEMBERS TO READ. THE NOTE STATED, "WE NOW HAVE THE PART TO MAKE AN ATOMIC BOMB." ONE OF THE MEMBERS ASKED JONES IF THIS WERE SO AND HE STATED, "YES, WE NOW HAVE THAT[."]

There's also a page containing a claim that should explain why I refused to accept what I considered blood money, or to undergo the therapy they offered survivors only if we admitted to having been brainwashed:

> [In] ADDITION, [Redacted] ALL THE SURVIVORS DEFINITELY NEED DEPROGRAMMING IN ORDER TO RETURN TO THIS SOCIETY AND TO PREVENT THEM FROM BECOMING DANGEROUS TO OTHERS OR TO THEMSELVES.

My FBI file includes at least four passages that refer specifically to Odell Rhodes's untrue accusation that I had been tasked with killing survivors:

> Odell Rhodes also told [redacted] [redacted] that HERBERT NEWELL and EUGENE SMITH (members of Lamaha Gardens) were not wanted on the plane returning to the United States because she [sic] (RHODES) heard that SMITH was ordered by STEVE JONES to kill survivors of Jonestown. . . .
>
> [Redacted] she feels members of the PT Church in San Francisco or members of the Jonestown basketball team would be the people that might try to harm the survivors of Jonestown. She also advised she heard that STEVEN JONES had given EUGENE SMITH instructions to kill all the survivors, although she didn't know if SMITH would carry these instructions out. . . .
>
> Concerning EUGENE SMITH, [redacted] he and the other returnees had heard that SMITH allegedly had the responsibility of killing himself and the other returnees and therefore did not want SMITH returning aboard flight 228 with them.
>
> When asked specifically about the original source of the allegations concerning SMITH, [redacted] advised that he could not furnish any further information, but that the word was that SMITH was given the responsibility of killing himself and the other church defectors. . . .
>
> [Redacted] he has no knowledge of a PT "hit list." [Redacted] at Georgetown he was told by STEPHANIE JONES that STEVE JONES told EUGENE SMITH to get rid of the defectors. [Redacted] the individuals he considered possible "hitmen" are STEVE JONES, CALVIN DOUGLAS, EUGENE SMITH, TERRY BUFFORD, and SANDY BRADSHAW.

In all the three hundred-plus pages of my FBI file, the only page that contains information that I consider true is the one listing my bare demographic information:

> The following information was obtained from discussion and observation:

Name	EUGENE [middle name] SMITH
Race	Negro
Sex	Male
Date of Birth (DOB)	July 29, 1957
Place of Birth (POB)	Detroit, Michigan
Height	Five feet six inches
Weight	185 pounds
Hair	Black
Eyes	Brown
Residence	(Prior March, 1978) – 1305 McAllister Street, San Francisco, California (1975) – 620 Buchannon [sic] Street, San Francisco, California
Occupation	Construction Worker, Free-Lance Photographer Arc Welder
Education	John O'Connel Trade School San Francisco, California Second Year College City College, Fresno, California
Marital Status	Married
Family Members	Wife – OLLIE MARIE WIDEMAN (Deceased) Son – MARTIN LUTHER SMITH, age five months, (Deceased)

FEDERAL BUREAU OF INVESTIGATION

RYMUR (JonesTown)

SUMMARY

PART # 1 of 1

PAGES AVAILABLE THIS PART 364

FD-302 (REV. 3-8-77)

b6
b7C

FEDERAL BUREAU OF INVESTIGATION

ALL INFORMATION CONTAINED
HEREIN IS UNCLASSIFIED
DATE 11/9/82 BY 1048 DKM/mkm

Date of transcription 1/4/79

An individual, who identified himself as EUGENE ERSKINE SMITH, was contacted as he departed Pan Am Flight 228 at John F. Kennedy International Airport (JFKIA), Queens, New York (NY). At this time, SMITH was advised of the identities of Special Agent (SA) [redacted] Federal Bureau of Investigation (FBI) and SA [redacted] United States Secret Service (USSS). SMITH was advised that the nature of the interview concerned the assassination of Congressman LEO RYAN and the activities of the People's Temple. (U)

SMITH indicated that his first affiliation with Reverend JIM JONES was in the early months of 1975, when his legal guardian, a [redacted] began attending meetings in Fresno, California. SMITH expalined that he attended for a few times but then stopped for approximately six months. He moved to San Francisco, California in late 1975 on Buchannon Street. SMITH would help with construction work at the People's Temple in San Francisco. He advised that he built a darkroom and a printing press. SMITH advised that during his initial indoctrination with the People's Temple, he often had doubts about JIM JONES' healings. SMITH advised that he went to the Jonestown settlement in March of 1978. He indicated that his wife, OLLIE MARIE WIDEMAN, had gone to Jonestown a week ahead of him. His mother had been there for six months. (U)

SMITH's only acknowledgement regarding written or oral oaths was that members would sign in at meetings. He said this was done because of the attempt on the life of JIM JONES. SMITH stated that he never signed anything. (U)

When questioned about whether JONES had personal bodyguards, SMITH only stated that JIMMY JONES, Jr., TIM GLEN JONES and JOHN COBB were always around him. (U)

SMITH advised that his duties in the Jonestown settlement included doing shoe repair work and being on the wood chopping crew. He stated that he lived in cottage number thirteen with his wife. SMITH could not recall the names of any other individuals who lived in cottage thirteen. SMITH (U)

Investigation on 12/29/78 at Queens, New York File # BO 89-495

by SA [redacted] /pm Date dictated 1/4/79

89-4286-1578

This document contains neither recommendations nor conclusions of the FBI. It is the property of the FBI and is loaned to your agency; it and its contents are not to be distributed outside your agency.

ENCLOSURE

FD-36 (Rev. 5-22-78)

FBI

TRANSMIT VIA:	PRECEDENCE:	CLASSIFICATION:
☐ Teletype	☐ Immediate	☐ TOP SECRET
☐ Facsimile	☐ Priority	☐ SECRET
☒ AIRTEL	☐ Routine	☐ CONFIDENTIAL
		☐ UNCLAS E F T O
		☐ UNCLAS

Date 12/28/78

TO: DIRECTOR, FBI
(ATTN: FBI Laboratory, Firearms Examination Section)

FROM: SAC, SAN FRANCISCO (89-250)(P)(Sqd. 4)

SUBJECT: RYMUR

DATE 11/9/92 b7C

Enclosed for the FBI Laboratory under separate cover are the following items: (U)

1. One ~~.38~~ 22 caliber revolver slug taken from the body of CHRISTOPHER LEWIS. (U)

2. One .38 caliber revolver slug taken from a wall of the house at 1447 Palou Street, San Francisco. (U)

3. One .22 caliber rifle slug taken from the living room wall of the house at 1447 Palou Street, San Francisco. (U)

4. [handwritten] Evidence from front of house at 1493 Palou Street (U)

For the information of the FBI Laboratory, CHRISTOPHER LEWIS, Negro male, date of birth 9/24/43, a former member of the People's Temple, San Francisco, California, was shot and killed on December 10, 1977. Removed from his body and from the crime scene were the enclosed projectiles. (U)

Through information developed in the San Francisco Division concerning the assassination of Congressman LEO RYAN, there have been allegations that the People's Temple may have been responsible for numerous criminal acts, including the murder of CHRISTOPHER LEWIS.

REC-47 89-4286-1605

(U)

23 JAN 15 1979

3 - Bureau (89-4286)
(1 Package Copy - Enc. 3)
2 - San Francisco (89-250
WJF/ddd
(5)

58 APR 2 1979
Approved: ________ Transmitted ________ (Number) (Time) Per ________

b6
b7C

BQ 89-495

indicated that on November 18, 1978, he was in Georgetown, Guyana, where he had been working for the past two months. His duties in Georgetown included working on the Bedford truck - unloading supplies. SMITH stated that he worked with CHUCK KIRKENDOLL and [redacted] He stated that both KIRKENDOLL and [redacted] were in San Francisco. During this time, he lived at the Lamaha Gardens in Georgetown. (U)

When asked about the Security Force, SMITH becamame increasingly vague with his answers. He provided the following names as being members of the Security Force (U)

TOM KICE
JIMMY JONES, Jr.
TIM GLEN JONES
JOHN COBB
TIM JONES (both white and black) (U)
LOU JONES

He advised that the Security Force "walked" with JIM JONES. SMITH stated that he never heard of the term "angels". (U)

SMITH indicated that he had only observed one weapon, a shotgun, and that they had a hunting license for it. SMITH did not supply any information about who and/or what was kept in hut number fourteen. It should be noted at this time that the interviewing Agent felt that SMITH was being evasive and deceptive. Continued inquiries regarding weapons and the Security Force met with negative results. (U)

PAGE TWO UNCLAS

PILOT REFUSED TO ALLOW A NUMBER OF OTHER MEMBERS OF PT ONTO AIRPLANE.(U)

BQMRA IN RECEIPT OF TELEPHONE CALL FROM (X) [redacted] (X), A PASSENGER ON PAN AMERICAN AIRLINES FLIGHT 228, WHO ADVISED THAT PT MEMBERS HAVE PLANS TO REGROUP IN THE UNITED STATES AND ARE DEFINITELY ANTI GOVERNMENT.(U)

b7C

NEWARK. INTERVIEW [redacted] TELEPHONE NUMBER [redacted] OR AT RESIDENCE, TELEPHONE NUMBER [redacted] (X), CONCERNING KNOWLEDGE OF PT MEMBERS ABOARD FLIGHT 228 AND OTHER PT MEMBERS WHILE IN GUYANA.(U)

RESULTS OF INTERVIEW SHOULD BE FORWARDED TO BUREAU, SAN FRANCISCO AND BQMRA.(U)

BT

#3322230-HQ 2

2

BQ 89-495

SMITH stated that he was never a member of the Planning Commission and only provided the names of TERRI BUFORD and TIM STOEN as being members. (U)

SMITH would not acknowledge any information regarding assassination plans or the forming of a "hit list". SMITH denied the fact that STEVEN JONES had given him assassination assignments. (U)

In regards to the death of SHARON AMOS and her three children, MARTIN, CRISTA and LE ANN, SMITH stated that he was not there. He was living at Lamaha Gardens. He advised that they were killed on November 18, 1978, their throats slit. SMITH stated that CHUCK BELKMAN and STEVEN JONES were being held for the deaths. SMITH indicated that STEPHANIE JONES was with the AMOS' at their deaths and that CALVIN DOUGLAS had pulled STEPHANIE JONES out. He stated that she also had a knife cut across her throat. SMITH denied that he had bragged about killing SHARON AMOS or that he had anything to do with their deaths. (U)

SMITH stated that he first heard of the deaths at the JONESTOWN settlement on November 19, 1978, when he was in Georgetown. SMITH said he later saw ODELL RHODES in Georgetown at the Park Hotel. According to SMITH, RHODES may have been responsible for holding children during the "forced suicides". (U)

Due to the fact that SMITH was being evasive and deceptive, the interview was terminated by the interviewing Agents. (U)

PAGE SIX NK 89-147 UNCLAS

ADDITION, [redacted] ALL THE SURVIVORS DEFINITELY 67C 67D

NEED DEPROGRAMMING IN ORDER TO RETURN TO THIS SOCIETY AND TO

PREVENT THEM FROM BECOMING DANGEROUS TO OTHERS OR TO THEMSELVES. (U)

BT

#

339

002

DEPARTMENT OF JUSTICE
FEDERAL BUREAU OF INVESTIGATION
COMMUNICATIONS SECTION

12-1-78 UNCLAS ROUTINE

*F002SRR AFOSDE HQ H0002 336*HSYUSR 020010Z DEC 78

FM DIRECTOR FBI (89-4286)

TO ALL SPECIAL AGENTS IN CHARGE

ALL INFORMATION CONTAINED HEREIN IS UNCLASSIFIED DATE 9/30/92 BY 1048 b7C

BT

UNCLAS

RYMUR

TO FACILITATE INTERVIEWS TO BE CONDUCTED REGARDING CAPTIONED MATTER, THE FOLLOWING IS A LIST OF SUGGESTED QUESTIONS WHICH SHOULD BE UTILIZED WHILE CONDUCTING INTERVIEWS (U)

1. DO YOU HAVE ANY SPECIFIC KNOWLEDGE OF AQUISITION, LICENSING, OR SHIPMENT OF ANY WEAPONS BY PEOPLE'S TEMPLE (PT) MEMBERS TO GUYANA OR ANYWHERE ELSE? (U)

2. DO YOU HAVE ANY SPECIFIC KNOWLEDGE OF FIREARM TRAINING RECEIVED BY PT MEMBERS INCLUDING SPECIFIC DATES, PLACES AND TRAINERS? (U)

REC-122 89-4286-713

3. ARE YOU AWARE OF ANY THREATS TO HARM PUBLIC OFFICIALS OR CURRENT AND FORMER MEMBERS OF THE PT AS A RESULT OF LEAVING THE CHURCH OR ATTEMPTS TO EXPOSE THE CHURCH AND (U)

22 DEC 5 1978

DO NOT TYPE ON PAGE BELOW THIS LINE

JEG:HAR 12-1-78 4047 b2

1 - MR. ADAMS
1 - MR. BOYNTON
1 - MR. MOORE
1 - MR. INGRAM
1 - MR. GOW
1 - MR. [redacted]
1 - MR. [redacted]

b7C

COMMUNICATIONS SECTION
DEC 02 1978

58DEC 8 1978

DO NOT FILE WITHOUT COMMUNICATIONS STAMP

102

1 2

12/1/78 UNCLAS E F T O IMMEDIATE

*F102Z00 AFOSDE HQ H0102 335*HSYESO 011928Z DEC 78

FM DIRECTOR FBI

TO ALL FBI FIELD DIVISIONS IMMEDIATE

BT

ALL INFORMATION CONTAINED
HEREIN IS UNCLASSIFIED
DATE ... BY ...

b7C

UNCLAS E F T O

RYMUR

FBIHQ IN RECEIPT OF TELETYPE FROM SECRETARY OF STATE WHICH STATES AS FOLLOWS: (U)

"REFERENCED TELEGRAMS AS WELL AS NEWS MEDIA COVERAGE CONCERNING THE GROUP KNOWN AS THE 'PEOPLES TEMPLE' HAVE STATED THAT THERE MAY HAVE BEEN OR INFERRED THAT THERE MAY STILL EXIST A PLAN TO ASSASSINATE THE PRESIDENT OF THE UNITED STATES AND ALL IN LINE OF SUCCESSION, OR TO ASSASSINATE/KIDNAP HIGH RANKING GOVERNMENT OFFICIALS. REC-122

THE DEPARTMENT OF STATE, OFFICE OF SECURITY, HAS THE PROTECTIVE RESPONSIBILITY FOR SECRETARY OF STATE CYRUS VANCE. TO MEET OUR RESPONSIBILITIES, IT IS REQUESTED THAT THE DOS, OFFICE OF SECURITY, BE NOTIFIED IMMEDIATELY OF ANY INFORMATION

89-4286-716

RDS/RAK (7) 12/1/78 5015/b b2

RDS

1 - MR. ADAMS
1 - MR. MOORE
1 - MR. INGRAM
1 - MR. GOW
1 - MR.
1 - MR.

b7C

FEDERAL BUREAU OF INVESTIGATION
COMMUNICATIONS SECTION

DEC 01 1978

DEC 5 1978

58DEC 8 1978

2

PAGE TWO DE HQ HQ102 UNCLAS E F T O

REGARDING THE SECRETARY, HIS OFFICE, OR ANY DEPARTMENT OF STATE EMPLOYEE, DURING THE ONGOING INVESTIGATIONS BEING CONDUCTED BY THE U. S. SECRET SERVICE/FBI."..

ANY OFFICES IN RECEIPT OF INFORMATION CONCERNING A THREAT TO SECRETARY OF STATE BY THE PEOPLES TEMPLE. IMMEDIATELY ADVISE FBIHQ SO THAT STATE DEPARTMENT CAN BE ADVISED. (U)

BT

#

FD-302 (REV. 3-8-77)

FEDERAL BUREAU OF INVESTIGATION

Date of transcription 1/3/79

[redacted] was presented with a subpoena to Testify Before Grand Jury in the United States District Court for the Northern District of California by Special Agent (SA) [redacted] on December 29, 1978. [redacted] is to appear in the Grand Jury Room, 17th Floor, 430 Golden Gate Avenue, San Francisco, California, on January 24, 1979, at 9:30 AM.

b3 Rule 6(e) + b7C

(U)

b7C

11/9/92

Investigation on 12/29/78 at Queens, New York File # BQ 89-495

by SA [redacted]/pm Date dictated 1/3/79

89-4286-1578

This document contains neither recommendations nor conclusions of the FBI. It is the property of the FBI and is loaned to your agency; it and its contents are not to be distributed outside your agency.

ENCLOSURE

BQ 89-495

b7C

[redacted] she feels members of the PT Church in San Francisco or members of the Jonestown basketball team would be the people that might try to harm the survivors of Jonestown. She also advised she heard that STEVEN JONES had given EUGENE SMITH instructions to kill all the survivors, although she didn't know if SMITH would carry these instructions out (U)

[redacted] while in Georgetown, she stayed at the Park Hotel. She advised they had to stay in Georgetown in order to testify at a hearing as to the facts surrounding what happened at the airport. When the time came, she advised it wasn't necessary for her to appear in court. She stated that [redacted] all testified at the hearing. (U)

[redacted] before leaving Georgetown, they were contacted by [redacted] of the United States Government, who had everyone fill out forms that we would repay the United States Government any money that they had spent on us. (U)

[redacted] she was glad to be out of Jonestown, and that she believed [redacted] would be going to a relative's home in [redacted] (U)

[redacted] following information about the below listed individuals she knew in Jonestown: (U)

Name	Position in Jonestown	Dead or Alive
TIM JONES, w/m	Security	Alive
JIMMY JONES, JR., b/m	Security	Alive
EDDY CRENSHAW, b/m	Truck and Tractor Driver	Dead

BQ 89-495

TERRY BUFORD

STEVEN JONES

TIM JONES

JOHN JONES

JOHN COBB

JIMMY JONES, JR.

CALVIN DOUGLAS

EUGENE SMITH

(U)

Concerning EUGENE SMITH, [redacted] he and the other returnees had heard that SMITH allegedly had the responsibility of killing himself and the other returnees and therefore did not want SMITH returning aboard flight 228 with them. (U)

b7C

When asked specifically about the original source of the allegations concerning SMITH, [redacted] advised that he could not furnish any further information, but that the word was that SMITH was given the responsibility of killing himself and other church defectors. (U)

[redacted] the following information concerning other PT church members or individuals affiliated with the PT church: (U)

TIM JONES - A leader of the Jonestown security force. (U)

BQ 89-495

Murder Targets (U)

No knowledge. (U)

Suicide Drills (U)

[redacted] heard that there were suicide drills conducted at Jonestown, but never participated in them. (U)

b7C

Relocation Plan (U)

No knowledge. (U)

Assassination Plan (U)

Unaware of any discussions regarding the assassination of Congressman LEO RYAN or the existence of an assassination squad. (U)

[redacted] Congressman RYAN was threatened by DON SLY with a knife while at Jonestown. (U)

b7C

ODELL RHODES also told [redacted] [redacted] that HERBERT NEWELL and EUGENE SMITH (members of Lamaha Gardens) were not wanted on the plane returning to the United States because she (RHODES) heard that SMITH was ordered by STEVE JONES to kill survivors of Jonestown. (U)

Radio (U)

The radio was used to call Lamaha Gardens at Georgetown and to order food and supplies. No knowledge of codes. (U)